FUTURE-PROOF YOUR WORKFORCE

DUA AL TOOBI

PASSIONPRENEUR®
PUBLISHING

FUTURE-PROOF YOUR WORKFORCE

Bridging the Divide Between
Nationalisation Goals and
the Digital Skills Gap in the GCC –
A Leader's Playbook

DUA AL TOOBI

Future-Proof Your Workforce
Copyright © 2025 Dua Al Toobi
First published in 2025

Print: 978-1-76124-223-6
E-book: 978-1-76124-224-3
Hardback: 978-1-76124-225-0

Publishing information
Publishing and design facilitated by Passionpreneur Publishing
A division of Passionpreneur Organization Pty Ltd
ABN: 48640637529

Melbourne, VIC | Australia
www.passionpreneurpublishing.com

This book is dedicated to the GCC's unwavering commitment to uplift and amplify the voices, aspirations, and achievements of women, forging a legacy of strength and progress in the land I proudly call home.

It is also lovingly dedicated to my late grandfather, Ghazi Mohamed Al Barwani, whose wisdom, nurturing, and profound commitment to service have deeply shaped my life. His legacy of kindness, perseverance, and service remains a guiding light that inspires my path.

And my mother, Nadia Ghazi Al Barwani, all I am is because of you, your strength and your love. This book stands as a testament to my voice and purpose, a tribute to the values they instilled in me and the transformative vision of the GCC.

ACKNOWLEDGEMENTS

This book owes its existence to the invaluable contributions of Moustafa Hamwi, Reim El Houni, Fahed Bizzari, and Corrina Cross. You have been instrumental in transforming my dream of becoming a published author from a mere idea into this tangible reality. I am deeply grateful for your support, mentorship, friendship, and contribution in accelerating my journey to authorship.

To George Harrak and Abdul Shakeel Aidarous, your exemplary leadership and the embodiment of its true essence have been both inspirational and aspirational. There are too few like you in the world. Your mentorship and friendship have been cornerstones of my career, and for this, I cannot thank you enough.

To the village that raised me: my mother, Nadia; my fathers, Abdallah and Najeeb; my grandparents, Shariffa and Ghazi (RIP); and my siblings – thank you for always accepting and encouraging me towards my dreams and goals; even when they seemed insurmountable, you only encouraged me with positivity and enthusiasm. Thank you for being my compass and guiding light in all the paths I've chosen.

To the siblings that I will always choose – Jawahir, Tope, Daisha, Faisal, Masha, Bashair, Anita, Aya, Said, Edina, Hussein, Mashail, and Manal – thank you for being the steadfast support system that has stood by me through thick and thin. Your love and support are my constant in my ever-changing world.

And to Saif AlQaizi Al Falasi (RIP) – simply, profoundly, thank you.

TABLE OF CONTENTS

INTRODUCTION

Transforming Potential into Power

'New technologies and approaches are merging the physical, digital, and biological worlds in ways that will fundamentally transform humankind. The extent to which that transformation is positive will depend on how we navigate the risks and opportunities that arise along the way.'

—KLAUS SCHWAB,
FOUNDER AND EXECUTIVE CHAIRMAN,
WORLD ECONOMIC FORUM

Have you ever found yourself at the intersection of old traditions and new technologies, witnessing the emergence of a new era? This book embarks on such a journey, especially focusing on the Gulf Cooperation Council (GCC) region. It's a narrative dedicated to you – the explorers, the leaders, and the forward thinkers eager to understand how culture intertwines with technology. Your role in guiding a region known for its rapid transformation and growth is crucial, and your efforts to drive resilience and innovation are deeply appreciated.

WHY THIS BOOK IS VITAL

This is not just another narrative on digital transition or national progress; it's a manifesto for profound organisational evolution and a guide for navigating tomorrow's complexities. It invites you to unlock the untapped potential within yourself and your organisation, preparing you for the future.

THE HEART OF THE STORY

What compelling story emerges when we talk about the digital future and nationalisation in the GCC? It's the narrative of integration – the concept that nationalisation and bridging the digital skills gap are not isolated activities, but intertwined efforts that are essential to transforming the region's competitive landscape. It's about leveraging human potential as the cornerstone of technological progress.

A SURPRISING DISCOVERY

In a landscape rife with challenges, set forth by the prevalence of the Fourth Industrial Revolution,[1] a surprising truth emerges: The solution to bridging the digital divide lies within our grasp. It's the realisation that every organisation possesses the capability to close the digital skills gap, not through external hires but by unleashing the potential of its existing workforce. The stunning reality is that the power to transform lies within, waiting to be harnessed.

ENVISIONING THE FUTURE

Picture a future where the rise of digital technology doesn't diminish traditional values but reinforces them. Imagine a world where bridging the digital skills gap creates a wealth of opportunities; where every individual, regardless of background or role, is empowered to embrace technology as a tool for growth and innovation. This book is your guide to

---

1   The Fourth Industrial Revolution (4IR) refers to a period of rapid technological advancements that integrate the physical, digital, and biological worlds, driven by innovations such as artificial intelligence, robotics, the Internet of Things (IoT), quantum computing, and biotechnology. This revolution builds on the digital infrastructure laid by the previous revolution, but it introduces entirely new capabilities, such as cyber-physical systems that enable interconnected smart machines and autonomous processes.

    According to Klaus Schwab, founder of the World Economic Forum, the 4IR represents a transformative shift, not just in industries but in society, fundamentally changing how people live, work, and relate to one another. Its impacts range from job displacement due to automation to the creation of new economic opportunities, while also raising challenges around inequality, security, and the nature of human identity.

envisioning and creating that tomorrow – a future where human potential is the driving force behind technological progress.

CREDENTIALS: A JOURNEY ROOTED IN PURPOSE AND EXPERTISE

With over a decade of leading major organizational transformations, my journey has centred on harmonising human potential with technological advancement. Starting my career in strategic execution roles and advancing to leadership positions in both Technology and Human Resources, I have gained unique insights into bridging the human–technology divide. This book is a reflection of that experience, aimed at demystifying the integration of national goals with digital skill development. It is driven by a deep commitment to democratising knowledge, aligning strategic objectives, and championing reskilling efforts to prepare the workforce for the future.

WHY I WROTE THIS BOOK

1. Unifying objectives: I've witnessed the tendency in my HR and tech career to treat digital transformation and national development as two separate organisational challenges. This book advocates for a unified approach, leveraging them as two sides of the same coin for organisational growth.

2. Democratising information: Stemming from my doctoral research, this book is solutions focused, sharing a wealth of global best practices, proven and successful interventions, as well as strategic frameworks to address the digital skills gap, intending to empower GCC corporations to future-proof their workforce.

3. Normalising reskilling: Throughout my career, the necessity of reskilling during organisational shifts has been evident. I advocate for a mindset that values adaptability. It is my strong belief that people are teachable, and so they should be hired for mindset and trained for skill, emphasising the potential within existing teams for innovation and growth.

WHAT THIS BOOK IS NOT

The following is not a theoretical discussion void of actionable solutions; it's a practical guide grounded in real-world experience and global best practices. It's not just a reflection of past achievements but a call to action for organisations to leverage their existing workforce as the catalyst for change.

Now that we are properly acquainted, let's get to work ...

CHAPTER 1

THE TURNING POINT

A Journey of Transformation in a Time of Change

WHY TRANSFORMATION MATTERS NOW

Transformation is no longer a lofty corporate ideal or distant goal – it's a fundamental necessity for survival and growth in today's volatile world. In the Gulf Cooperation Council (GCC), this truth has never been clearer. The region's bold aspirations to diversify economies, embrace cutting-edge technologies, and cultivate local talent present immense opportunities. Yet, these aspirations also bring challenges that demand visionary leadership and decisive action.

This book is the culmination of my journey – one that began in strategy, evolved through dual leadership roles in HR and technology, and now continues as a consultant and advisor advocating for digital transformation and workforce reskilling across the region. Along the way, I've led transformations that reshaped industries, economies, and lives. I've also faced personal trials that redefined my purpose and passion, propelling me toward a mission to contribute to the GCC's growth during its most transformative era.

Through this book, I aim to demystify transformation, offering practical solutions and real-world insights for leaders navigating this critical juncture in history.

From Strategy to Transformation

My career began in the dynamic world of aviation, where strategy wasn't just an abstract concept – it was the driving force behind the success of complex global systems. At Etihad Airways, the UAE's national airline, I was tasked with translating the organization's ambitious vision into actionable strategies across its diverse divisions, including the integration of internationally acquired subsidiaries.

I quickly learned that transformation isn't about imposing change but weaving it into the fabric of an organization. One of my most formative experiences came when I relocated to Switzerland to integrate European carriers acquired by Etihad. Operational alignment was challenging, but it was the human dynamics – cultural differences, competing priorities, and divergent visions – that required the most care. These experiences reinforced a vital truth: Transformation begins with people. Processes and systems are important, but their success hinges on aligning the individuals who make them work.

People at the Heart of Change

Realising that people are the cornerstone of every successful transformation led me to pivot toward HR, where I managed some of the most impactful projects of my career. One such initiative was leading the UAE's first three-way banking merger, a landmark event that reshaped the financial landscape of the country. This wasn't just a logistical challenge – it was a deeply human endeavor. It required uniting cultures, fostering trust, and managing the uncertainties of thousands of employees, stakeholders, and communities.

These experiences taught me that transformation requires empathy as much as strategy. Success isn't just about meeting targets; it's about empowering people – making them feel seen, valued, and capable of contributing to a shared vision. This belief, that empowered people drive successful change, became the cornerstone of my leadership philosophy.

Technology: The Catalyst for Growth

While people remained my focus, I became increasingly fascinated by the transformative power of technology. It was clear to me that the 21st century would be defined by digital innovation, and I committed myself to staying ahead of this shift. Pursuing an Executive Master in Digital Transformation, I became the first GCC national to earn this distinction, equipping myself with the tools to navigate the intersection of technology, leadership, and strategy. Later, I deepened this expertise through my Doctorate of Business Administration (DBA), where my research focused on future-proofing the GCC's workforce amid rapid technological change.

This journey reached a pivotal moment at Al Hilal Bank, where I served in dual leadership roles across HR and technology. As Director of Digital Transformation and part of the team leading the establishment of the UAE's first digital Islamic bank, I witnessed how technology could reshape industries and redefine customer experiences. However, I came to understand that technology itself wasn't the transformation – it was the way it united processes, empowered teams, and enabled a vision for the future. Technology isn't the destination; it's the catalyst that empowers people to achieve more.

A PERSONAL TRANSFORMATION

Transformation isn't just professional – It's deeply personal. During the COVID-19 pandemic, I faced a health crisis that would change my life. A genetic condition compounded by the virus left me in intensive care, fighting for survival. Told I might never walk again, I was forced to confront my own mortality. But this period of adversity also brought clarity: If I emerged from this challenge, I would dedicate myself to something greater.

As I recovered, I paused my DBA research to focus on turning those insights into actionable contributions for the region.

This book is the result – a bridge between my personal experiences, my professional journey, and the challenges and opportunities I see in the GCC. It is a playbook for leaders navigating digital transformation, nationalisation, and workforce reskilling, offering practical frameworks and real-world strategies to drive meaningful change.

Why This Book, Why Now

The GCC is undergoing a seismic shift. Economies are diversifying, workforces are evolving, and technology is transforming the way we live and work. Yet, these opportunities are accompanied by significant challenges: bridging the digital skills gap, aligning nationalisation efforts with global innovation, and ensuring that transformation serves people as much as profit. This book is my contribution to that critical moment.

Through this journey, I've also embraced advocacy. As a member of the global nonprofit Women in AI, I've witnessed the power of inclusion and diversity in driving innovation. These values are reflected throughout this book. Too often, transformation is presented as an abstract ideal, cloaked in complex theories. This book breaks through that noise. It's for the leader struggling to align technology with strategy, the HR leader looking to empower local talent, and the policymaker seeking actionable solutions for the digital age. It's a guide to turning challenges into opportunities and making transformation not just possible but inevitable.

The Call to Transform

Transformation isn't just about technology, strategy, or people—it's about all three working in harmony to create a future worth striving for. For me, this journey is deeply personal. It's rooted in my career, my health, and my passion for empowering the GCC to navigate its future with confidence.

The pages ahead are more than a roadmap; they are an invitation to lead boldly, adapt fearlessly, and embrace the opportunities of a rapidly changing world. Whether you are a leader navigating disruption, an entrepreneur seizing new opportunities, or an individual looking to future-proof your career, this book is for you.

The question is no longer whether transformation is necessary. The question is: Will you step forward and lead it?

CHAPTER 2

THE DIGITAL RENAISSANCE

Harnessing Technology and Tradition
to Shape the GCC's Future

THE DIGITAL AGE MEETS TRADITION

In a world defined by rapid technological disruption, the Gulf Cooperation Council (GCC) finds itself at a pivotal juncture. With a rich cultural heritage and vast technological potential, the region is uniquely positioned to navigate a delicate balancing act: integrating transformative technologies while preserving its identity and traditions. This chapter explores how the GCC can actively embrace this digital renaissance, not as passive adopters of global trends but as leaders in defining a future where technology drives economic growth, national resilience, and cultural preservation.

The GCC is no stranger to reinvention. Once reliant on oil, its economies are now pivoting toward diversification and sustainability. This transition, accelerated by national ambitions like Saudi Vision 2030, Oman Vision 2040 and the

UAE's Fourth Industrial Revolution strategy, underscores the urgency of marrying technological advancements with national priorities such as workforce nationalisation and knowledge-based economy building. Yet, this path is fraught with challenges that require visionary leadership and a commitment to fostering both innovation and inclusion.

The Landscape of Challenges

The journey to digital leadership in the GCC is marked by complexities that demand strategic alignment, innovative thinking, and cultural sensitivity. Among the most pressing challenges are:

1. The Digital Skills Gap

- The rapid pace of technological advancement has outstripped the region's current workforce capabilities. Bridging this gap is essential to unlocking the full potential of digital transformation.
- Training and reskilling programs must be prioritised to empower local talent and equip them with future-ready skills, from data analytics and AI to cybersecurity and blockchain.

2. Nationalization and Global Expertise

- Balancing the empowerment of national workforces with the integration of global expertise is a critical challenge.

Both are necessary for fostering innovation while ensuring local ownership of economic progress.

- Governments and organizations must develop strategies that leverage international partnerships while building robust local ecosystems of talent and innovation.

3. Cultural Harmony

- Technology adoption must align with the region's deep-rooted cultural values. The GCC's approach to digital transformation must reflect its identity, ensuring that innovation enhances rather than erodes its traditions.

4. Economic Diversification

- Moving beyond an oil-centric economy requires targeted investments in technology-driven sectors such as fintech, renewable energy, healthcare, and smart cities.
- Policymakers and business leaders must adopt a holistic view of economic development, integrating digital solutions to drive sustainability and inclusivity.

NATIONALISATION AS A CATALYST FOR TRANSFORMATION

For too long, nationalisation policies in the GCC have been treated as isolated mandates—checklists to meet quotas rather than engines of progress. This book challenges that narrative, presenting nationalisation as a dynamic force that, when seamlessly integrated with digital transformation, can drive profound corporate and economic advancement. When nationalisation shifts from a compliance exercise to a strategic imperative, it becomes a powerful lever for innovation, inclusivity, and sustainable growth.

At its heart, nationalisation is about more than developing skills; it's about fostering representation. A visionary, digital-first national leader doesn't just lead with technological expertise—they embody the aspirations of a society poised for the future. By building pathways for others to follow, they create a ripple effect, cultivating a generation of empowered professionals who carry forward the same ethos of innovation and progress. This is the recipe for building knowledge-based societies: a foundation of empowered leaders equipped with both cutting-edge tools and a deep connection to their cultural identity.

Central to this vision is the commitment to upskilling and reskilling the workforce—cultivating a culture of continuous learning that empowers national talent to adapt and lead in a rapidly changing technological landscape. By embedding these advancements into the fabric of nationalisation efforts, the GCC can create a workforce that not only reflects its cultural heritage but also positions the region as a beacon of innovation in the global digital economy. Nationalisation, when redefined and driven by representation, becomes the cornerstone of transformation—not just for organizations, but for the societies and legacies they shape, ensuring a future where talent and technology work in harmony to drive progress and prosperity.

Shifting the Narrative

Nationalization has often been perceived as a compliance-driven initiative, with organisations meeting quotas without fully leveraging the potential of local talent. This mindset must shift. Nationalization, when paired with digital transformation, becomes a powerful tool for unlocking untapped potential, fostering innovation, and driving sustainable growth.

The key lies in integrating nationalisation into a broader organizational strategy. This involves:

- Reskilling for the Future: Providing GCC nationals with the skills and tools needed to thrive in digital-first environments.
- Redefining Leadership: Building a new generation of leaders who understand the interplay between technology and tradition.
- Fostering Collaboration: Creating ecosystems where national and global talent work together to innovate and grow.

A Roadmap for the GCC's Digital Renaissance

This chapter serves as a roadmap for leaders navigating the complexities of the GCC's digital transformation. It provides a structured approach to addressing the dual challenges of nationalisation and technological advancement while ensuring that cultural values remain central to progress. The roadmap unfolds as follows:

1. Understanding the Foundations

- Delve into the challenges of the digital skills gap and the evolving role of nationalisation in the GCC.
- Examine the region's historical reliance on oil and the imperative to diversify.

2. Explosive Interactions

- Analyze how nationalisation and digital transformation can complement each other, creating opportunities for synergistic growth.

3. Navigating Technological and Skillset Evolution

- Identify the pivotal technologies reshaping industries, from AI and blockchain to renewable energy and smart infrastructure.
- Highlight the skills needed to harness these technologies effectively.

4. Crafting Strategy

- Formulate actionable strategies that marry global best practices with the GCC's unique cultural and economic landscape.

5. Understanding Human–Technology Synergy

- Emphasise the integration of technology with human capabilities, focusing on workforce empowerment and innovation.

6. Future-proofing for Sustainability

- Advocate for agile, sustainable strategies that enable continuous adaptation to change.

7. Synthesising and Acting

- Offer a consolidated action plan to guide leaders through this transformative era.

A Vision for Tomorrow

The GCC's digital renaissance is about more than economic growth; it's about shaping a future where technology and tradition coexist harmoniously. This vision requires bold leadership, a commitment to inclusion, and an unwavering focus on fostering local talent. By addressing the digital skills gap, redefining nationalisation, and embracing a holistic approach to transformation, the GCC can emerge as a global leader in the digital age.

The journey ahead is not without challenges, but it is filled with opportunities to redefine what is possible. As we continue through this book, each chapter will build on these themes, providing a comprehensive playbook for navigating this transformative era. Together, we can chart a future that honors the GCC's past while embracing the limitless potential of its tomorrow.

CHAPTER 3

UNDERSTANDING NATIONALISATION IN THE GCC

Nationalisation in the GCC is more than a policy – it's a reflection of regional aspirations, history, and the vision for the future. A journey from humble beginnings to powerful modern economies, nationalisation isn't just about quotas. It embodies empowerment, sustainability, and regional identity. This chapter delves into the essence of nationalisation within the GCC, tracing its roots, motivations, and the many factors that have shaped it.

HISTORICAL CONTEXT

The historical journey of nationalisation in the GCC starts long before the establishment of these nations. The Arabian Peninsula, traditionally home to Bedouin tribes, was marked by simple economies revolving around pearl diving, fishing, and nomadic herding. The rhythm of life was dictated by nature: seasons, the desert, and the sea.

But the 20th century brought about a tectonic shift with the discovery of oil. From being primarily agrarian societies, GCC nations transformed into global energy powerhouses, attracting a wave of expatriate talent. This rapid modernisation and influx of foreign expertise highlighted a crucial issue: the underrepresentation of the local population in key sectors of their booming economies.

The realisation led to the birth of nationalisation policies, initially focusing on employment quotas for local citizens. However, these policies evolved, transitioning from mere employment numbers to holistic strategies emphasising education, vocational training, and entrepreneurship. This shift underscored the understanding that true nationalisation is not just about jobs but building future-ready, diversified, and knowledge-based economies.

As the landscape transformed, so did the cities. With burgeoning oil revenues, urban development projects led to cities like Dubai and Riyadh evolving from modest towns to global metropolises. By the turn of the 21st century, visionary diversification projects, such as Saudi Arabia's Vision 2030, the UAE's Vision 2021, and the Sultanate of Oman's Vision 2040 emerged, focusing on reducing oil dependence, fostering innovation, and ensuring the active participation of the local populace.

Evolution of nationalisation

The journey of nationalisation saw a growing emphasis on supporting small-to-medium enterprises (SMEs) and digital literacy. Governments began forming partnerships with educational institutions and businesses to create curriculums reflecting the demands of the modern workplace. Scholarships became prevalent, and entrepreneurial incentives were launched, ensuring the regional vision aligned with empowerment, capability, and capacity-building.

Digital transformation became central to nationalisation in the new age. Initiatives such as the 'One Million Arab Coders' in the UAE aimed to train young Arabs in computer programming. Efforts were intensified to ensure equal digital access, recognising its crucial role in ensuring inclusive growth. The trajectory of nationalisation remains dynamic, adapting to regional needs, global trends, and national ambitions.

Influences shaping nationalisation

The journey of nationalisation in the GCC has been influenced by a myriad of factors:

- Economic diversification: Recognising oil as a finite resource, GCC countries have been striving to diversify their economies, thus aligning nationalisation policies with non-oil sectors.

- Demographic dynamics: A youthful population meant a pressing need to provide adequate employment opportunities and guidance to the new generation entering the workforce.
- Global events: The 2008 financial crisis emphasised the need for self-reliance, triggering a re-evaluation of nationalisation policies. Similarly, the COVID-19 pandemic accelerated digital transformation and highlighted the importance of a tech-savvy local workforce.
- Visionary goals: National visions, such as Saudi Arabia's Vision 2030 and Oman's Vision 2040, emphasise the role of empowered local citizens in shaping the future, thus moulding nationalisation policies to encompass entrepreneurship, digital literacy, and sustainable development.

In summary, nationalisation in the GCC, influenced by both internal and external factors, is poised to navigate the challenges and opportunities of the 21st century, aiming for prosperity, inclusivity, and sustainability for its citizens and residents.

GLOBAL VIEW: SINGAPORE'S SKILLSFUTURE

With a global lens, we can see striking similarities outside of the GCC. Singapore's SkillsFuture initiative offers valuable insights into the concept of national talent development and how a nation can systematically bridge skills gaps. It serves as a poignant example of how forward-thinking policy frameworks can significantly impact a nation's workforce.

Overview: SkillsFuture is a national movement initiated in 2015 to provide Singaporeans with the opportunities to develop their fullest potential throughout life, regardless of their starting point. The initiative recognises the challenges of a rapidly changing global landscape and seeks to equip its citizens with skills relevant for the future.

Key components

- SkillsFuture Credit: Every Singaporean above the age of 25 receives an opening credit, which can be used to offset course fees for a wide range of skills-related courses.
- SkillsFuture Earn and Learn: A work–learn program designed specifically for new graduates, enabling them to deepen their skills in jobs related to their field of study.
- SkillsFuture Fellowships: Awards for Singaporeans to achieve mastery in their respective fields, supporting their advanced skills training.
- SkillsFuture Advice: Community outreach events that aim to guide individuals in their skills development journey and career planning.

Outcomes: Singapore has witnessed increased participation in continuous learning initiatives, with many Singaporeans taking advantage of the credits to upskill or reskill. The emphasis on lifelong learning has helped in fostering a culture where skill development is a continuous journey, rather than a one-off effort.

Relevance to nationalisation: The SkillsFuture model underscores the importance of a holistic approach to workforce development. Rather than merely focusing on quotas or reservations, the emphasis is on empowering the entire population with the skills and knowledge needed for the future. This proactive approach ensures that the workforce remains agile and adaptable, ready to take on the challenges of a rapidly evolving global landscape.

Key takeaways: While the socioeconomic and cultural contexts differ, the SkillsFuture initiative offers a best-practice perspective on how to approach workforce development comprehensively. It highlights the importance of cross-industry and cross-sector collaboration:

- Government support: Strong government backing, both in terms of policy framework and financial support, is vital.
- Holistic approach: Beyond just job placement, the focus should be on continuous learning, reskilling, and upskilling.
- Public–private partnerships: Collaboration between the government, educational institutions, and the private sector can lead to more relevant and impactful training programs.

Singapore's SkillsFuture is a testament to what is possible with holistic commitment to human capital development. While the challenges faced by the GCC might differ, the principles remain the same: A proactive, comprehensive, and inclusive approach to workforce development can yield transformative results.

REGIONAL VIEW: SAUDI ARABIA'S VISION 2030

One of the most visionary and transformational national initiatives in the GCC region, Saudi Arabia's Vision 2030 serves as a strategic roadmap that seeks to reshape the Kingdom's socioeconomic landscape, reducing its dependence on oil revenue and diversifying its economy. With an emphasis on nationalisation and human capital development, it provides pertinent insights for any discussion on nationalisation efforts in the GCC.

Overview: Introduced in 2016 by Crown Prince Mohammad bin Salman, Vision 2030 is Saudi Arabia's blueprint for the future. It revolves around three primary themes: a vibrant society, a thriving economy, and an ambitious nation. The plan seeks to harness the country's strategic location, its youthful population, and its rich Islamic heritage to achieve its objectives.

Key components related to nationalisation

- Increased employment: Vision 2030 seeks to reduce unemployment and raise women's participation in the workforce.
- Sectoral diversification: Focusing on sectors beyond oil, like tourism, entertainment, and technology, to create new employment avenues for Saudis.
- Education reform: Revamping the educational system to align with market demands and international standards, with an emphasis on skills relevant for the future.
- Nitaqat system enhancement: While the Nitaqat system was introduced before Vision 2030, its principles have been further integrated and enhanced under the new vision, with more defined targets and a broader scope.

Outcomes: Since its inception, Vision 2030 has driven several reforms, from opening up the Kingdom to international tourism to changes in women's rights and participation. On the nationalisation front, there's been a notable increase in the participation of Saudi nationals in the private sector and a shift in the sociocultural narrative towards embracing modern industries and roles.

Relevance to bridging the digital skills gap: Vision 2030 acknowledges the importance of a digitally proficient workforce in achieving its objectives. Efforts to enhance digital infrastructure, promote technology startups, and introduce digital skills in educational curriculums signify a commitment to bridging the digital skills gap.

Saudi Arabia's Vision 2030 showcases how national visions, when executed with clarity and commitment, can drive significant change in both economic and social spheres. For leaders in the GCC region, it acts as a testament to the importance of long-term planning, stakeholder engagement, and adaptive execution in achieving nationalisation goals while fostering a digitally proficient workforce.

The success of a leader in harmonising nationalisation goals with the demands of the digital era lies in their ability to strategise, execute, and adapt. This book provides a holistic roadmap, ensuring that leaders are equipped to make informed decisions that both serve the national interest and bridge the digital skills gap for the entire workforce in order to achieve a unified approach to achieving and sustaining organisational growth.

As we conclude our exploration of the dynamic landscape of nationalisation in the GCC – a landscape rich with historical context, evolving policies, and visionary goals – we stand at the threshold of another equally pivotal and challenging arena: the digital skills gap. Moving to Chapter 4, we confront a critical byproduct of this transformational journey – the widening gap between existing digital competencies within our workforce and the global market's rapidly evolving technological demands.

CHAPTER 4

THE DIGITAL SKILLS GAP

In the globalised and interconnected world of today, the digital skills gap has emerged as one of the most pressing challenges faced by organisations. As the landscape of technology continuously evolves, so too do the skills required to navigate and harness its potential. This chapter explores what constitutes the digital skills gap, analysing its origins, manifestations, and implications for businesses and economies.

DEFINING THE DIGITAL SKILLS GAP

The digital skills gap refers to the disparity between the digital skills required in the workforce and the actual skills possessed by its workers.

At its core, the digital skills gap is a mismatch, a discord between demand and supply. On one side of the equation, we have the demand – businesses and economies that increasingly rely on digital technologies needing a workforce adept at navigating the digital landscape. They seek professionals capable of leveraging technology to innovate, improve efficiency, and deliver value to customers. They require coders, data scientists, artificial intelligence (AI) specialists, and cybersecurity experts; but equally critical are professionals across all sectors who possess a robust foundational understanding of digital technologies and the expertise to leverage technology for competitive advantage in the business landscape across industries.

On the other side, we have the supply – individuals entering or already part of the workforce, many of whom lack the necessary digital competencies. While many are proficient users of digital applications and surface-level technologies, their skills often fall short when it comes to leveraging these technologies in a professional setting, understanding their strategic implications, or innovating with them.

In the middle of this mismatch, we find the digital skills gap. It's a gap that varies in size and nature, depending on the specific context. For some industries, it might mean a scarcity of high-level tech specialists, like AI experts. For others, it might be a lack of professionals with intermediate digital skills, like data analysis or digital marketing. And for the workforce at large, it often translates into a deficiency in basic digital literacy – the foundational skills needed to use digital technologies effectively and safely.

The digital skills gap, however, is not just a static, one-dimensional problem. It's a dynamic, multifaceted challenge. It evolves with technological advancements, shifts with changes in the labour market and industry-specific changes, and is shaped by a host of factors, from education and training systems to socioeconomic conditions and policy landscapes.

In the context of the GCC, the digital skills gap is of particular relevance. Amid ambitious digital transformation and nationalisation initiatives, the digital skills gap stands as both a challenge to be overcome and an opportunity to be seized. Understanding this gap in its full complexity is crucial to forging a path towards a future where technology empowers economies, enriches societies, and enables individuals to reach their full potential.

SIGNIFICANCE AND IMPACT OF THE DIGITAL SKILLS GAP

In the era of the Fourth Industrial Revolution, where digital technologies permeate almost every aspect of our lives – shaping how we work, communicate, and interact with the world – there is a mismatch between the digital skills that the current and future workforce possesses and the skills that the evolving economy requires. This digital skills gap is substantial and growing, and this divide separates those equipped to flourish in the digital age from those who are not.

At the core of the digital skills gap is the exponential pace of technological evolution. From AI and machine learning (ML) to blockchain and data analytics, technology is reshaping the economic landscape at an unprecedented rate. This rapid change necessitates a workforce adept in navigating and leveraging these technologies. However, the reality is that many individuals, businesses, and even entire nations find it challenging to keep up with the pace of change. This is not only to gain a competitive advantage but also as a matter of survival and business continuity for a demographic of changing consumer needs in the height of the digital era, leading to the growing relevance of a digital skills gap.

It's crucial to understand that the digital skills gap is multifaceted. It spans a wide spectrum of abilities, from basic digital literacy, such as using digital tools for communication and information retrieval, to advanced technical skills, such as programming, cybersecurity, and data analysis. Furthermore, the gap also encompasses 'soft' skills, including digital leadership, digital collaboration, and the capacity to adapt to digital transformation. These skills are becoming increasingly important as organisations undergo digital transformation.

While the digital skills gap is a global issue, its manifestations and impacts vary significantly across regions, industries, and demographic groups. The interplay between technological development and socioeconomic factors, such as education, income level, and age, often exacerbate the digital skills gap, leading to significant disparities within and between nations.

Addressing the digital skills gap is imperative. Left unbridged, this gap could stifle economic growth, exacerbate social inequalities, and hinder organisations' abilities to innovate and compete. On the other hand, successfully bridging the digital skills gap can fuel economic development, improve social mobility, and empower individuals and businesses to thrive in the digital age.

In the context of the GCC, understanding and addressing the digital skills gap is crucial. Given the region's young age, sustainability requirements after the oil boom, as well as nationalisation policies, digital transformation goals, and the ability to bridge the digital skills gap, can be significant factors in determining the region's future trajectory. With this understanding, we embark on a deeper exploration of the digital skills gap in the GCC, including why it's so significant and what exactly the impact will be if we ignore it.

- Economic impact: The digital skills gap has profound implications for economic growth and competitiveness. The digital economy thrives on innovation and productivity enhancements, both of which rely on a skilled workforce. When businesses can't find employees with the necessary digital competencies, they struggle to develop new products, improve efficiency, and adapt to market changes, stifling their growth and the broader economy.
- Social inequality: The digital skills gap also exacerbates social inequalities. Those with advanced digital skills command higher salaries and have better job prospects, while those lacking such skills often find themselves marginalised. This digital divide can widen socioeconomic disparities, leading to the 'haves' and the 'have-nots' of the digital age.

- Organisational resilience: In a business landscape where disruption is the norm, digital dexterity is key to organisational resilience. Companies need employees who can leverage technology, adapt to changes, and drive digital transformation. A workforce ill-equipped with necessary digital skills hampers organisations from responding effectively to industry shifts, making them vulnerable to disruption and loss of market share to more digitally savvy competitors.
- National security: The digital skills gap also has implications for national security. As cyber threats become increasingly sophisticated, countries need skilled professionals to safeguard their digital infrastructure. A lack of such experts can leave nations exposed to cyberattacks, with devastating consequences.
- Future readiness: The future is undeniably digital-first. As AI, machine learning (ML), and other advanced technologies become commonplace, digital skills will be non-negotiable. Bridging the digital skills gap is essential to prepare the workforce for the jobs of the future and ensure the society's overall readiness for future technological advancements.

In the context of the GCC, these implications take on added weight due to the region's ongoing efforts to diversify their non-oil-related gross domestic product (GDP) and subsequent nationalisation and digital transformation agendas. The significance of the digital skills gap is thus intricately woven into the narrative of the region's future. Recognising this significance is the first step towards crafting effective strategies to address the gap and harness opportunities the digital era brings.

GLOBAL IMPACT AND CONSEQUENCES OF THE DIGITAL SKILLS GAP

Globally, the broader narrative is clear: The world is racing towards a digital future, but a significant proportion of the global population lacks the digital skills to keep pace. According to the World Economic Forum's *Future of Jobs Report 2025*, 39% of workers' current skill sets are expected to be disrupted or outdated by 2030. This ongoing transformation threatens to widen social inequalities, hinder economic growth, and limit the full potential of digital progress. Yet, within this gap lies immense opportunity — for innovation, inclusion, and advancement — if we choose to bridge it with strategic foresight and bold, coordinated action.

The tremors of the digital skills gap echo throughout the world, manifesting in profound and far-reaching consequences. At a global scale, these consequences shape economies, societies, and even geopolitics, painting a complex and compelling narrative of our digital age.

Economic impact

On an economic level, the digital skills gap can act as a speed bump on the superhighway of digital transformation. When businesses struggle to find the skilled digital talent they need, their ability to innovate and compete is undermined. According to a study by Korn Ferry, by 2030, talent shortages in key sectors could result in about US$8.5 trillion in unrealised annual revenues globally (see 'The $8.5 Trillion Talent Shortage').

For economies as a whole, the digital skills gap can exacerbate structural inequalities. As digitally skilled workers command higher salaries, income disparities can grow, fostering economic imbalances. Countries that fail to bridge their digital skills gaps risk being left behind in the global digital economy, with their growth prospects dimmed by the shadows of digital exclusion.

Social impact

The digital skills gap also has significant social implications. It can deepen societal divisions, creating a 'digital divide' between those with digital skills and access, and those without. This divide can exacerbate social inequalities, impede social mobility, and limit access to opportunities. For example, those without digital skills may find it increasingly difficult to access essential services, find jobs, or participate fully in their communities, as more and more aspects of life move online.

Geopolitical impacts

On a geopolitical scale, the digital skills gap influences power dynamics and competition. Countries with robust digital skills ecosystems can gain a competitive edge, leading in innovation, influencing the trajectory of digital technologies, and dominating entire industries. They can export their digital products and services, shaping global digital norms and standards. Meanwhile, countries that lag behind risk becoming consumers rather than creators of digital technologies, with their digital destinies shaped by others.

Environmental impacts

Moreover, the digital skills gap can have environmental impacts. As industries worldwide struggle to meet the demand for digital skills, there's a surge in energy consumption and electronic waste, which can contribute to environmental degradation. On the flip side, if addressed properly, the digital transformation – driven by closing the digital skills gap – could lead to more sustainable practices. For instance, the development and deployment of technologies for renewable energy, resource management, and circular economies heavily depend on the availability of digital skills.

As we stand on the threshold of a future increasingly defined by digital technologies, these consequences of the global digital skills gap underscore the urgency and significance of our collective efforts to bridge it. Every person empowered with digital skills is a step towards a more inclusive, vibrant, and sustainable digital future.

THE DIGITAL SKILLS GAP IN THE GCC

The GCC is no different to our global neighbours facing the ramifications of the Fourth Industrial Revolution; the digital skills gap in the region is an intricate issue influenced by a complex interplay of factors and compounded by the nuances of our cultural history and bespoke labour market. Just as the natural forces shape the landscapes, there are key elements that contribute to the emergence of this skills gap:

1. Rapid technological evolution: The fast-paced nature of technological advancements often exceeds the adaptability of educational systems and the workforce in the GCC. The continuous requirement for adaptation poses a significant challenge for both institutions and individuals.

2. Misalignment between education and market demands: There is a notable discrepancy between the academic curriculum and the practical skills demanded by the labour market due to the constant evolution of technology. The educational institutions might not be sufficiently focused on imparting the skills and competencies that are essential for a modern digital workforce, leading to graduates being inadequately prepared.

3. Reliance on an expatriate workforce: The GCC has traditionally relied on a workforce from outside the region, particularly in specialised fields. This dependence is further exemplified by the acquisition of global tech talent, which may contribute to the insufficient focus on

developing the skills and competencies of the local population as organisations focus primarily on the necessity to survive in the changing business landscape.

4. Perceptions of career prestige: Certain societal perspectives within the GCC may not regard careers in technology and digital sectors as being as prestigious as traditional professions such as medicine, engineering, banking, and law. This viewpoint may discourage potential talent from venturing into digitally related careers and exploring the possibilities of the future of these industries with a strong foundation in digital competencies.

5. Inadequate corporate training and development: The culture of continuous learning and employee development in digital skills may not be sufficiently established in some organisations within the GCC. The lack of comprehensive training programs leaves the workforce less equipped to tackle emerging digital challenges. Additionally, GCC corporate training has been theory-based, rarely with the opportunity to apply those learnings. A large part of the digital skills of the future would require application-based and vocational training to provide hands-on experience to fully grasp the skills to be used in the workforce.

6. Regulatory obstacles and bureaucracy: Regulatory environments in the GCC might not be evolving as rapidly as the technological landscape. The bureaucratic procedures can slow down the implementation of educational

programs and corporate training initiatives, and impede the attraction of international digital talents.

7. Lack of synergy among stakeholders: Addressing the digital skills gap demands a collaborative approach involving governments, educational institutions, corporations, and individuals. There has been a tendency toward fragmented and siloed efforts that do not maximise the collective potential of all stakeholders.

8. Limited accessibility to cutting-edge technologies and resources: Despite the GCC's wealth in resources, accessibility to the latest technologies and educational resources may be restricted for the local population, particularly in less urbanised areas. This limitation hampers the cultivation of practical skills.

9. Preference for formal certifications over practical skills: There is a cultural perception and practice to prioritise formal certifications and degrees over hands-on experience and practical skills. This emphasis sometimes results in qualifications that do not correlate with the competencies needed in practice.

10. Global competition for talent: The GCC is not alone in its pursuit of digital talent. There is a worldwide demand for such skills, and the GCC must compete with other regions that might be offering more attractive incentives or opportunities.

11. Entrepreneurial ecosystem: Innovation is cultivated in a supportive environment for startups and entrepreneurs; without this, economies can impede the growth of innovative businesses and solutions within the region.

12. Language barriers: With much of the educational material and resources in technology being in English, language barriers might impede the ability of certain segments of the population to acquire digital skills effectively and at speed if Arabic-based tech education is not made accessible.

13. Quality of digital infrastructure: The adequacy and reliability of digital infrastructure, such as internet connectivity and access to modern hardware, can also be a determining factor. In some areas, suboptimal infrastructure can hinder learning and application of digital skills.

14. Attitudes toward lifelong learning: Cultural attitudes toward continual learning and self-improvement may play a significant role. If lifelong learning is not ingrained and encouraged by organisations and educational institutions alike, professionals might be less inclined to update their skills as technology evolves.

15. Awareness and perception of digital careers: There might be a lack of awareness or understanding of the full range of career opportunities available in the digital sector,

which prevents individuals from recognising and pursuing these options.

16. Integration of digital skills in K–12 education: The introduction of digital skills training at an early age is crucial. The absence of digital literacy and critical thinking in primary and secondary education can lead to a less prepared workforce.

17. Public–private partnerships: The lack of collaboration between the government and private sector in formulating strategies for digital skills development and pathways for applying the newly learnt skills can also widen the digital skills gap.

18. Migration policies and retention strategies: Policies that do not facilitate the retention of foreign talent or the return of nationals who have studied abroad might contribute to a brain drain and the loss of an opportunity to cultivate the digital leaders of the future, which can exacerbate the digital skills gap both in the short and long term.

19. Adaptation to remote work and global collaboration: As remote work becomes more prevalent, the ability of the workforce and organisations to adapt to remote collaboration tools and practices is crucial. Failure to adapt may cause a gap in skills necessary for the modern global work environment, and the subsequent lack of ability to compete with organisations that possess that agility. The lack of organisational flexibility in the digital age has proven

to be one of the largest drivers of attrition, as we are see-ing to date as part of the great resignation.

It is important to recognise that the digital skills gap is a dynamic and multifaceted issue being faced on a global scale and, while the GCC's combination of drivers for this are largely nuanced by our rich culture, they are also influenced by the organisational cultures and norms of the industries that shape our economy. A holistic approach that considers all these factors and encourages collaboration among stake-holders will be key to addressing this challenge in the GCC and pave a pathway toward innovation, economic prosper-ity, and establishing the region as a leader in the digital age. The integration of modern education, adaptive policies, and inclusive cultural perspectives is vital in this transformative journey.

THE RAMIFICATIONS OF THE SKILLS GAP FOR GCC ECONOMIES

As the region that has been the cradle of civilisations and the nexus of trade for centuries, the GCC now stands at a cross-roads. The modern economic landscape, deeply interwoven with digital technologies, presents monumental opportunities as well as challenges. One such challenge is the digital skills gap, the ripple effects of which are significant and complex:

1. Curtailed innovation and global competitiveness: The digital skills gap can act as a bottleneck for innovation

within the GCC. The absence of a workforce proficient in contemporary digital competencies may restrain companies from keeping pace with global counterparts, impacting technological progress and diminishing global competitiveness.

2. Obstacles in economic diversification: The GCC has been actively pursuing economic diversification to reduce dependence on oil and gas revenues. However, the skills gap may prove to be a hurdle, as emergent sectors like renewable energy, fintech, and e-commerce are intrinsically linked to digital prowess.

3. Reliance on foreign talent: The skills gap can lead to an over-reliance on international expertise. While foreign talent can bring valuable skills, excessive dependence can be economically unsustainable and may result in capital outflows as professionals remit earnings to their home countries.

4. Influence on unemployment rates: The local populace, particularly the youth, may face heightened unemployment levels due to the digital skills gap. As industries evolve with technological advancements, the dearth of relevant skills can pose significant barriers to employment for local job seekers.

5. Diminished foreign direct investment (FDI): For foreign investors, the calibre of the local workforce is a critical determinant in investment decisions. The perceived

inadequacy in digital skills may render the GCC less appealing for FDI, as investors may be concerned about the availability of skilled human resources.

6. Inefficiencies in public sector services: The public sector's effectiveness is contingent on the digital acumen of its workforce. The skills gap may lead to inefficiencies, protracted processing times, and a failure to meet the evolving expectations of citizens for digital services.

7. Vulnerability to cybersecurity risks: As digital transformation accelerates, cybersecurity becomes increasingly critical. The skills gap, particularly in cybersecurity, can expose GCC economies to heightened risks associated with cyberattacks, potentially impacting critical infrastructure and financial integrity.

8. Exacerbation of socioeconomic disparities: The skills gap can contribute to widening socioeconomic inequalities. Individuals with access to digital education may prosper, while those lacking such access might find themselves increasingly marginalised, lacking the ability to get access to services and struggling to find opportunities for employment.

9. Escalating costs for talent acquisition: The digital skills shortage may force companies to incur higher costs in training and talent acquisition, which can have downstream effects on profitability and consumer pricing.

10. Challenges to workforce nationalisation initiatives: The skills gap can impose constraints on workforce nationalisation endeavours. The absence of a skilled local talent pool can complicate the fulfilment of nationalisation targets without compromising the necessary digital competencies if organisations are not willing to develop their newly acquired national employees with digital skills.

In this intricate mosaic of economic ramifications, it is imperative that the GCC harness its storied heritage of adaptation and ingenuity. Through dedicated focus, strategic planning, and collaboration among stakeholders, the GCC has the opportunity to address the digital skills gap. This is not just a challenge to be surmounted, but an opportunity to lay the groundwork for a sustainable and robust digital economy that can propel the region into a future of prosperity and global leadership.

GLOBAL BEST PRACTICE: FINLAND'S DIGITAL PROWESS

In addressing challenges, it is often valuable to turn to global examples that showcase both the pitfalls to avoid and the strategies that have yielded success. This section will shine a spotlight on a specific global instance that illustrates the nuances of the digital skills gap, offering insights and takeaways that can be applied in various contexts.

FIGURE 1. FINLAND'S DIGITAL PROGRESS PROGRAM

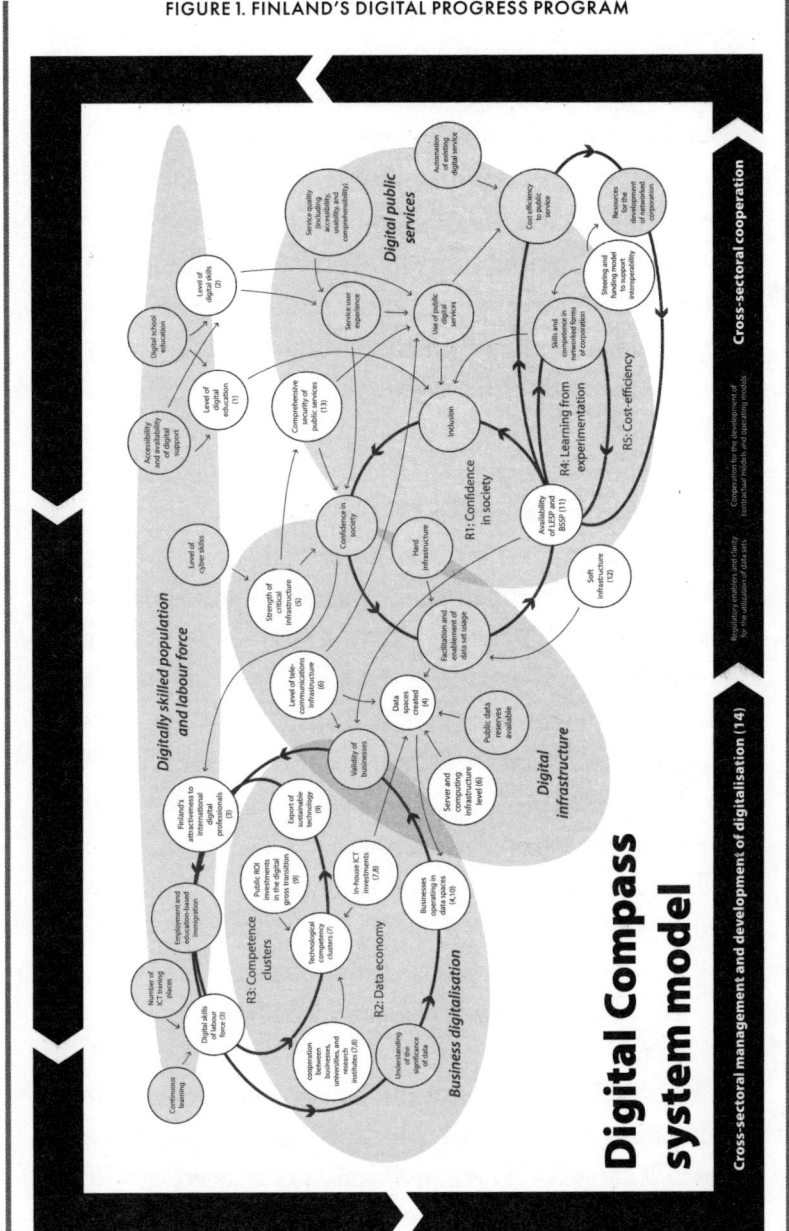

Background

Finland's success in digital skills proficiency is not solely attributed to its education system and industry partnerships. The country has also shown commendable efforts in reskilling its citizens who already possess information and communication technology (ICT) skills, thereby creating a dynamic talent pipeline that adapts to technological advancements. An exemplary initiative in this regard is the TechSkillsAtlas.

Government initiatives

In addition to integrating digital skills into education curriculums, the Finnish government has recognised the importance of reskilling the existing workforce. The TechSkillsAtlas initiative is a prime example of this strategy. This initiative identifies individuals with ICT skills but potentially outdated knowledge and equips them with the latest skills demanded by the tech industry (Business Finland).

The TechSkillsAtlas initiative

The TechSkillsAtlas initiative is a targeted approach aimed at harnessing the potential of individuals who possess foundational ICT skills. These individuals may need upskilling to align with the rapidly evolving tech landscape. Through this initiative, the government collaborates with tech companies, educational institutions, and industry associations to identify the specific skills in demand.

Key features of TechSkillsAtlas

- Skills assessment: The initiative begins with a comprehensive assessment of participants' existing ICT skills. This assessment helps identify areas where individuals may require upskilling.
- Tailored training: Based on the assessment, personalised training pathways are designed. These pathways focus on developing the skills that are currently in demand by the tech industry.
- Industry collaboration: TechSkillsAtlas involves collaboration with tech companies to ensure that the training provided is aligned with real-world industry needs. This collaboration enhances the employability of participants upon completing the program.
- Recognition and certification: Upon successful completion of the training, participants receive recognition and certification, validating their updated skills. This serves as a valuable asset when seeking new employment opportunities or career advancements.
- Continued learning: The initiative emphasises the importance of continuous learning. Participants are encouraged to stay engaged with evolving technologies and trends to remain competitive in the job market.

Creating a new talent pipeline

By focusing on reskilling individuals with existing ICT skills, Finland's TechSkillsAtlas initiative effectively creates a new talent pipeline that is attuned to the needs of the tech industry. This approach not only addresses the digital skills gap but also taps into the latent potential of individuals who can contribute meaningfully to the evolving digital landscape.

Key takeaways for leaders, organisations, and policymakers in the GCC

Holistic approach to talent development

Finland's TechSkillsAtlas initiative showcases that talent development should encompass both nurturing new talent and upskilling existing employees. This holistic approach helps create a versatile and adaptable workforce.

Collaborative efforts

Partnerships between governments, tech companies, and educational institutions can yield remarkable results in bridging the digital skills gap. Collaborating with industry experts ensures that training remains relevant and aligned with industry demands.

Recognising potential

Leaders and organisations should recognise the untapped potential within their workforce. Initiatives like TechSkillsAtlas demonstrate that individuals with foundational skills can be transformed into valuable contributors through targeted upskilling.

Continuous learning

Encouraging a culture of continuous learning within the organisation is essential. CEOs should inspire employees to stay updated with technological advancements, enabling them to remain competitive and agile.

Finland's TechSkillsAtlas initiative showcases the country's commitment to reskilling its citizens with existing ICT skills, contributing to a responsive talent pipeline. By leveraging partnerships, personalised training, and recognition, this initiative exemplifies how nations and organisations can proactively address the digital skills gap and remain competitive in the digital era. CEOs, organisations, and policymakers can draw valuable insights from such initiatives to create a workforce that's equipped for ongoing success.

Now that we've completed our comprehensive analysis of the digital skills gap in Chapter 4, we encounter the vital intersection where this gap meets the GCC's objectives of nationalisation in Chapter 5. This is where we shift our focus from diagnosing the challenges to exploring actionable strategies and synergies. It's a narrative that moves from understanding a global phenomenon to applying this understanding in a regional context, setting the stage for leaders to forge a path that harmoniously aligns the aspirations of nationalisation with the imperatives of the digital era.

INTERSECTION OF NATIONALISATION AND DIGITAL SKILLS

As the GCC strives to achieve nationalisation goals, it's imperative to understand that this ambition doesn't exist in a vacuum. The landscape is intricately tied to the digital realm, with its myriad opportunities and challenges. This chapter delves deep into the confluence of nationalisation objectives and the imperatives of bridging the digital skills gap, examining how they intertwine, conflict, and potentially complement each other.

THE DUAL CHALLENGE

In the evolving landscape of global business, leaders, particularly those in the GCC, find themselves navigating two paramount challenges: the push for nationalisation and the need for digital competence. Here, we deconstruct the intricacies of this dual challenge and explore its multifaceted dimensions.

Nature of the challenges

- Sociopolitical impetus of nationalisation: At its core, nationalisation is not just an economic agenda but is deeply entwined with the sociopolitical fabric. It aims to reduce dependency on expatriate labour, promote local talent, and ensure that nationals play a pivotal role in their economy.
- The inescapable digital revolution: In parallel, the Fourth Industrial Revolution has made it abundantly clear that digital proficiency is no longer optional. It's the lifeblood for the survival and competitiveness of organisations in virtually every sector.

The push-and-pull dynamics

- Nationalisation quotas vs. digital skill gaps: As organisations race to meet nationalisation targets, they also grapple with a simultaneous shortage of specific digital skills within the entire talent pool as well as the national talent pool. This dichotomy often places organisations in a challenging position.
- Local relevance vs. global competitiveness: While nationalisation emphasises localising the workforce and solutions, digital transformation often requires global standards, tools, and strategies. Striking a balance becomes essential.

Operational implications

- Talent acquisition: Firms might find that while there's ample local talent available for certain roles, especially in highly nationalised sectors such as banking, there's a deficit when it comes to specific digital roles like AI specialists or data scientists, similar to the wider talent population.
- Talent retention: Beyond hiring, the challenge extends to retaining talent. As the local workforce becomes more digitally skilled, they become attractive prospects for the wider market and become targeted by the competition, potentially leading to higher turnover rates.
- Training and development: The dual mandate necessitates robust training programs, not just in terms of upskilling for digital roles but also in terms of developing long-term career paths that are fit for purpose for the cultural and strategic importance of nationalisation.

Strategic implications

- Long-term vision: Leaders must ensure that while immediate nationalisation targets are met, the long-term vision of a digitally proficient organisation isn't compromised and that nationalisation strategies are encompassed in the overall digitalisation strategy.
- Budgetary considerations: Investments need to be made both in hiring and training local talent and in digital

tools, technologies, and infrastructure. This dual financial commitment requires careful budgeting and resource allocation.

- Stakeholder management: Managing the expectations of stakeholders, from government bodies to shareholders, becomes crucial. Transparent communication about the challenges and progress becomes essential.

Potential conflicts

Mismatch in skill availability and organisational needs

- Scope of expertise: While nationalisation might drive organisations to onboard local talent, there might be a mismatch between the available skillsets in the national workforce and the specific digital competencies required by the organisation.
- Rapidly evolving digital landscape: The digital world is continuously evolving, and today's critical skills might become obsolete tomorrow. While nurturing local talent, it becomes challenging to keep pace with the shifting digital paradigm.

Cultural differences in workplace dynamics

- Traditional values vs. digital flexibility: Local cultural norms might emphasise hierarchy and traditional ways of working. Conversely, the digital landscape often thrives on agility, flexibility, and flatter organisational structures. Merging the two can be challenging.

- Perceptions about technology: In certain cultures, there's a tangible apprehension about technology replacing jobs or eroding cultural values. These perceptions can hinder the adoption of digital tools and practices.

Regulatory and policy challenges

- Nationalisation quotas: Stringent quotas might force companies to hire local talent even when they're not the perfect fit for certain roles, leading to inefficiencies in the long term or longer onboarding times.
- Digital policy limitations: There might be local regulations that limit certain digital operations, from data storage to the use of particular technologies, further complicating the marriage of nationalisation and digital transformation.

Economic implications

- Cost impediments: Training local talent to meet the digital demands might sometimes be more cost-intensive than hiring ready-made talent from the global market. Balancing the economic implications with nationalisation objectives can be challenging if not viewed through the lens of long-term sustainability.
- Growth vs. localisation: While localisation can bring about sustainable long-term growth, in the short term,

companies might face growth hindrances as they divert resources towards building local digital competencies.

Talent mobility concerns

- Retention challenges: As local talent is upskilled and becomes more digitally proficient, it becomes attractive to international companies, leading to potential 'brain drain' scenarios.
- Limitations in global talent acquisition: Nationalisation objectives might restrict firms from tapping into the global talent pool, even when certain skills are critically needed and not readily available locally.

Understanding the dual challenge is the first step toward crafting informed strategies. While the potential conflicts are multifaceted, they aren't insurmountable. By recognising these challenges, leaders can proactively design strategies and frameworks that not only anticipate these conflicts but also craft pathways to navigate them effectively. While nationalisation and digitalisation might seem at odds, they represent two sides of the same coin – a coin that, when flipped skilfully, can lead to unparalleled long-term organisational success and societal progress. The goal is to ensure that both nationalisation and digital transformation objectives amalgamate in a manner that benefits the organisation and the nation.

MAPPING THE CHALLENGES

In the convergence of nationalisation and digital evolution, there lies an intricate web of challenges that leaders must navigate. These challenges are multifaceted, spanning from policy hurdles to the practicalities of implementing digital strategies while promoting nationalisation goals. Understanding these challenges is the first step toward crafting effective solutions. This section provides a detailed map of these hurdles, setting the stage for subsequent discussions on strategies and solutions.

The speed of digital evolution

As the world finds itself propelled into an era dominated by digital innovations, the velocity of this evolution becomes a significant point of contention, especially when contrasted with nationalisation goals. The rapid advancement of technology has reshaped industries, economies, and even societies. However, the speed of digital evolution poses specific challenges, particularly in regions like the GCC, where nationalisation agendas and workforce development objectives must be met.

Rapid technological advancements

Today's cutting-edge technology can become tomorrow's legacy system, such is the speed of tech development. From the onset of the internet era in the 1990s and the transition to mobile computing in the 2000s to the current landscape dominated by AI, blockchain, and the Internet of Things (IoT), the pace of technological advancements has been nothing short of meteoric. This speed creates a constant race for organisations to keep up, adapt, and stay relevant.

- Innovation lifecycles: Traditional innovation lifecycles that allowed businesses several years to adopt, adapt, and maximise new technologies are now significantly compressed. Companies find themselves needing to pivot or upgrade their Tech Stack continuously, leading to increased operational pressures and costs.
- Consumer expectations: As technology advances, so do consumer expectations. Businesses find themselves in a position where they need to constantly update their services and products to meet the fast-evolving demands of their digital-savvy customers.

LEGACY SYSTEMS

While new technologies emerge at a blistering pace, many organisations, especially those that have been operational for decades, grapple with legacy systems. These older systems, tools, and protocols often become deeply embedded in an organisation's operations, creating inertia against change.

- Integration challenges: Incorporating new digital tools or platforms with existing legacy systems can be a complex, time-consuming, and often expensive endeavour. It requires not just technical solutions but also a retraining of staff and a reshuffling of operations.

- Operational risks: Transitioning away from legacy systems carries operational risks. Data migration, potential downtime, or even loss of critical information are challenges that organisations must navigate carefully.
- Cultural resistance: Legacy systems are not just technological but can also be cultural. Employees accustomed to a certain way of working might resist changes, viewing new digital tools with suspicion or apprehension related not just to their skills but also their job security.

Mismatch between digital progress and training

The speed at which new digital technologies emerge and evolve can outpace the rate at which training programs are designed and implemented. This misalignment can lead to a workforce that, although trained, might not be equipped with the most current or relevant digital skills.

- Continuous learning imperative: For organisations, this rapid evolution underscores the importance of fostering a culture of continuous learning, where training isn't a one-off event but an ongoing journey.
- Dynamic curriculum: Training programs, especially those aimed at nationals in the context of the GCC, must be dynamic. They need to be regularly updated to reflect the current technological landscape, ensuring that

trainees are being equipped with skills that are immediately relevant and applicable.

- Ineffective traditional training: Traditional corporate training programs are ineffective in the digital revolution as traditional training programs for corporations, whether external or in-house, have been designed to provide learners with the technical knowledge but are not accompanied with a mechanism for the learners to apply what they have learnt within their jobs or organisations. The acquisition of new skills must be accompanied with the opportunity to be applied within projects or new job responsibilities for the learners to achieve mastery, thus normalising a continuous learning culture.

The speed of digital evolution, while offering numerous opportunities, presents a layered set of challenges for businesses and policymakers. Balancing the demands of rapid technological change with the imperatives of nationalisation requires strategic foresight, agility, and a commitment to continuous learning and adaptation, as well as to implementation. Understanding the nuances of this rapid evolution is crucial for leaders looking to navigate the intersection of nationalisation and the digital skills landscape effectively.

Skill development lag

In an era where the digital landscape evolves daily, skill development within the workforce becomes paramount. However, the dynamic nature of technology often means that there's a dissonance between the skills available in the market and the ones in high demand. This disparity, termed the 'skill development lag', is an intricate challenge, especially when nationalisation goals are in play.

Mismatched training

The foundations of the skill development lag often lie in mismatched training. As technology forges ahead, training programs, curriculum, and educational institutions may not keep pace, leading to a workforce that's skilled, just not in areas that are immediately relevant.

- Reactive vs. proactive curriculum: Traditional training programs often respond to current market needs rather than anticipating future ones. This reactive approach can mean that by the time a cohort completes their training, the skills they've acquired might already be outdated.
- Lack of industry–academia collaboration: A crucial element leading to mismatched training is the lack of synchronicity between the corporate world and academia. Without constant dialogue and collaboration, educational institutions might not be in tune with the real-time needs of industries.

Duration of skill acquisition

Acquiring a new skill, especially in nuanced technological domains, isn't instantaneous. The time taken for training, combined with the time it takes for individuals to gain proficiency and mastery, can lead to significant lags.

- Rapid technology turnover: Some technologies have a brief lifespan of dominance. By the time an extensive training program on such a technology concludes, the industry might have already moved on to the next big thing.

- Depth vs. breadth: The balance between gaining a broad understanding of various technologies versus deep expertise in one technology is tricky. The duration of acquiring in-depth knowledge might be long, but specialisation can also lead to niche expertise that may not be in widespread demand.

External factors influencing skill demand

It's not just the pace of technology that impacts skill demand. External factors such as geopolitical shifts, global economic trends, and even pandemics can reshape the skill landscape unexpectedly.

- Economic fluctuations: Economic downturns or booms can lead to shifts in skill demands. For instance, economic challenges might accelerate digital transformation efforts, leading to a sudden spike in demand for digital skills.
- Policy changes: Government policies, especially those related to technology, trade, or education, can influence which skills become crucial. A new policy promoting, say, data localisation might lead to an increased demand for professionals skilled in data centre management within a region.

Skill development lag is not just a challenge but an indicator of the broader dynamics at play between education, technology, and market demands. For leaders, understanding this lag is crucial, not just for workforce development but also for broader strategic planning.

The imperative is clear: to foster an agile, adaptive, and forward-looking approach to skill development that is attuned to the rapid shifts of the digital age and the intricacies of nationalisation. The objective of this book is to provide you with a framework to future-proof your workforce to achieve this imperative.

Cultural and perception challenges

Navigating the confluence of nationalisation goals and the increasing demand for digital proficiency necessitates an understanding that transcends technicalities and enters the realm of culture and perception. Cultural attitudes and prevailing perceptions can significantly influence the uptake of digital skills and the success of nationalisation initiatives.

Cultural views on digital careers

In many regions, including parts of the GCC, certain professions and fields of study have historically held prestige. These fields may overshadow emerging digital domains, creating a reluctance among the younger generation to pursue careers in tech.

- Traditional prestige professions: Fields like medicine, engineering, and law have conventionally been deemed prestigious. The rapid rise of digital careers might not have yet gained the same societal endorsement, making them less attractive options for many.

- Lack of visible role models: One of the factors perpetuating these cultural views is the absence of prominent local figures in the tech world. Visible role models who have forged successful digital careers can inspire others to pursue similar paths.

Perceptions around skill acquisition

Misconceptions about the nature of digital skills can be a significant barrier. Common misconceptions include the notion that digital skills are exceedingly complex, reserved for a 'tech-savvy' elite, or not suitable for those from non-tech backgrounds.

- Overemphasis on technical skills: While technical proficiency is vital in the digital world, technical skills can be learnt; however, soft skills like problem-solving, critical thinking, and collaboration are equally essential. The narrative needs to shift to highlight the holistic nature of digital roles to emphasise the transferable skills people already possess to be able to pivot their careers and reskill into a tech role.
- Age-related stereotypes: There's a common stereotype that digital skills are a domain for the younger generation. This misconception can deter older employees from upskilling or reskilling, feeling that they might not be suited for the digital era.

Lack of representation of Khaleeji women in tech

In the nexus of nationalisation ambitions and digital skill demands, cultural attitudes and perceptions play a pivotal role. As organisations endeavour to shape a future-ready workforce, the importance of female representation cannot be overstated.

- Human–technology interplay: As the digital landscape evolves, it becomes increasingly evident that empathy, emotional intelligence, and a holistic understanding of human needs are crucial. These qualities are not exclusive to any gender but are often associated with strengths that women bring to the table. A workforce that values and integrates these attributes can navigate the complex interplay between technology and humanity with greater agility.

- The perception challenge: Female representation becomes a strategic imperative when considering the perception challenge. Visible representation of women in leadership positions and roles traditionally dominated by men serves as a powerful narrative. It dismantles preconceived notions about what is achievable, inspiring young women to envision themselves as vital contributors to the digital future. Organisations that prioritise female representation send a clear signal that diverse participation is not just a token gesture but a genuine commitment to reshaping the perception of who belongs in the digital workforce.

Cultural resistance to change

At an organisational level, deeply entrenched corporate cultures can resist the adoption of digital methodologies. This resistance isn't just a technological issue but is rooted in deeper cultural and behavioural norms within the organisation.

- Fear of redundancy: Employees might resist digital transformation efforts out of fear that automation and digital tools might render their roles redundant.
- Hesitation to abandon legacy systems: Beyond the technical aspects, employees might have a sentimental or trust-based connection to older systems, viewing new digital tools with apprehension or mistrust.
- Communication barriers: Inadequate communication from leadership about the need, benefits, and strategies for digital transformation can exacerbate cultural resistance.

Cultural and perception challenges are multifaceted, with roots in historical, societal, gender, and organisational dynamics. Addressing them requires a multi-pronged approach that includes awareness campaigns, education, and robust leadership communication. For organisational leaders, understanding and addressing these cultural nuances can be the difference between successful and unsuccessful nationalisation and digital transformation initiatives.

Resource constraints

Bridging the gap between nationalisation and digital skills acquisition will naturally encounter resource constraints. In an era where the demand for digital skills outpaces supply, organisations must contend with limitations not just in capital but in human resources, time, infrastructure, and more.

Financial limitations

Digital transformation, while an investment, requires significant upfront capital. The immediate costs of procuring new technologies, training staff, or hiring new talent can be prohibitive for some companies.

- High costs of cutting-edge technology: Implementing the latest digital solutions, whether AI, blockchain, or advanced data analytics tools, can be expensive. While they promise a long-term return on investment (ROI), the initial outlay can be a deterrent.
- Training and upskilling costs: Investing in continuous training for staff to ensure they remain relevant in their roles demands financial resources, both for training programs and potential downtime during training sessions.

Talent scarcity

The fast-evolving digital landscape means that certain skills become valuable almost overnight, leading to a talent market where demand heavily outstrips supply.

- Competition for talent: Organisations aren't just competing within their industries but across sectors for the same pool of digital talent. This can drive up salaries and make talent acquisition a costly endeavour.
- Retention challenges: Even after successful talent acquisition, the high demand for digital professionals means companies face challenges in retention. Without the right incentives, growth opportunities, and work culture, talent may easily migrate to competitors or different sectors.

Time constraints

The urgency to digitise and adhere to nationalisation mandates often means organisations are racing against time.

- Quick technological evolution: The pace at which technology evolves necessitates almost immediate adoption and adaptation. Organisations may find it challenging to keep up, especially if the internal training and development processes are not sufficiently agile. Organisations need to prioritise creating flexible learning environments and reskilling programs that can be rapidly deployed to meet the needs of an ever-changing technological landscape. This ensures that their workforce remains capable and prepared, allowing the organization to seamlessly integrate new technologies and methodologies without falling behind in their strategic objectives.
- Infrastructure barriers: Beyond software and talent, the physical infrastructure to support digital operations can be a constraint.

- Legacy systems: Many organisations operate on older IT infrastructures that aren't compatible with newer digital tools. Migrating from these systems can be both time-consuming and expensive as opposed to starting from a less technologically advanced baseline.
- Nationalisation timelines: Governments may set strict timelines for nationalisation targets. Meeting these timelines while also ensuring that the workforce is digitally competent can be a juggling act.
- Lack of physical infrastructure: Especially in areas that are still developing, there may be a lack of necessary physical infrastructure such as robust internet connectivity, data centres, and more.

Resource constraints present tangible barriers in the journey of marrying nationalisation and digital competency development. Addressing these constraints requires strategic planning, creative problem-solving and, at times, external partnerships and collaborations. Leaders need to take a holistic view, considering not just immediate needs but the long-term sustainability and scalability of their digital and nationalisation strategies.

OPPORTUNITIES AND SYNERGIES

Amid the challenges of aligning nationalisation and digital skill requirements, there lies a silver lining of synergies and opportunities waiting to be harnessed. Recognising and capitalising on these intersections can propel an organisation's success and drive both mandates forward simultaneously.

Tapping into local digital talent

- Emerging digital natives: Members of the younger generation, often referred to as digital natives, have grown up in the age of technology. Nationalisation can leverage this homegrown talent who inherently understand both the local cultural context and the digital landscape.
- Local innovators: There's a surge in local entrepreneurs and tech enthusiasts developing solutions tailored to regional needs. Incorporating these innovators can bring fresh perspectives and innovative solutions to organisations.

Public–private partnerships (PPPs)

- Joint ventures for skill development: Collaborative ventures between government entities and private businesses can lead to specialised training institutes, harnessing both policy support and industry knowledge.
- Digital infrastructure projects: Governments looking to boost their digital economies might invest heavily in infrastructure. Private companies can play pivotal roles in these projects, from providing technology solutions to training human resources.

Localised and bespoke
digital education and training

- Tailored curriculum: Collaborations between corporations and educational institutions can lead to courses specifically designed for regional digital needs, combining global tech knowledge with local applicability to industry and workforce.
- On-the-job training: Internships, apprenticeships, and continuous on-the-job training can be tailored to equip local employees with the most relevant and up-to-date digital skills.

Fostering an innovation ecosystem

- Innovation hubs: Creating spaces where local talent can brainstorm, innovate, and develop digital solutions can foster a culture of tech entrepreneurship and innovation.
- Local tech competitions and hackathons: Hosting or sponsoring tech events can identify and nurture local digital talent, simultaneously pushing for digital innovation tailored to regional needs.

The intersection of nationalisation and the digital skills gap isn't just a space of challenges but one brimming with untapped potential. By recognising the inherent synergies and opportunities, leaders can craft strategies that don't just meet mandates but drive their organisations into a future of sustained growth, innovation, and regional relevance.

NAVIGATING THE INTERSECTION

At the crossroads of nationalisation and digital transformation, organizations face significant challenges: resource constraints, talent scarcity, skill development gaps, budget limitations, and a rapidly evolving digital landscape. These roadblocks can seem overwhelming, especially when trying to maintain a competitive edge in a changing market. Mastering this intersection requires a nuanced understanding, strategic planning, and the ability to align these dual objectives into a cohesive roadmap. It is clear that current human capital development structures are no longer fully equipped to bridge these gaps effectively.

The evolution of workforce development

In the ever-changing landscape of nationalisation and digital transformation, traditional human capital development methods have shown signs of inefficacy.

The following illustration depicts the organisational and employee effort for the entire national workforce in typical GCC corporations.

FIGURE 2.

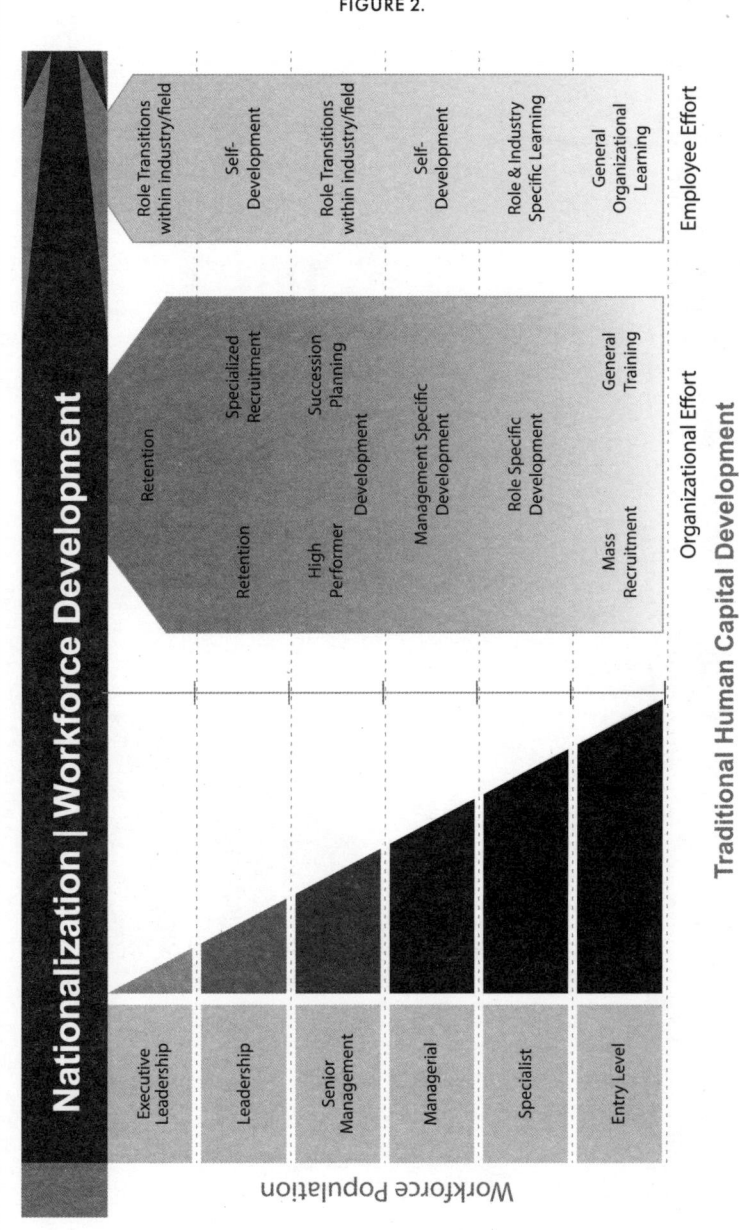

FIGURE 3.

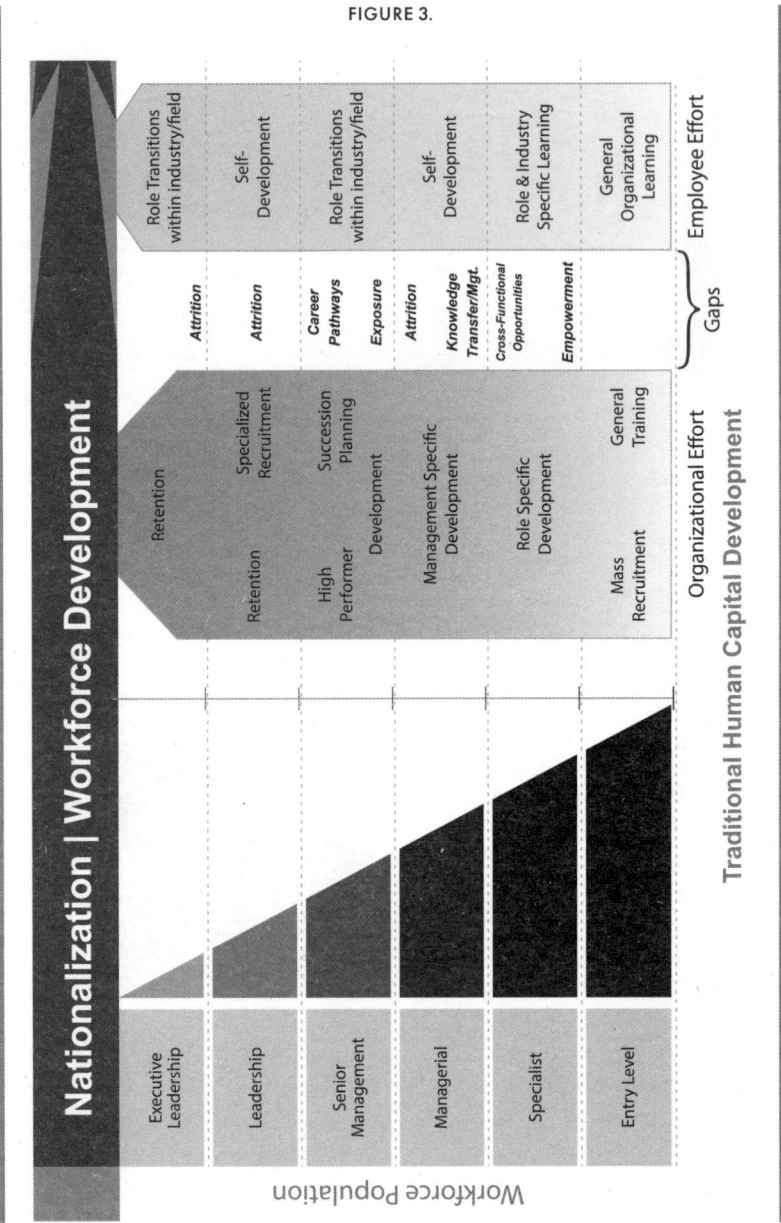

The above illustration further exemplifies the gaps in human capital development that results in lack of engagement and ultimately attrition of nationals as they progress in their career within an organisation. Let's delve deeper into this matter to comprehend the challenges inherent in the formulation of workforce development frameworks that can future-proof our workforce.

Entry level

Traditionally, nationals are often recruited through mass recruitment drives such as graduate programs for entry-level positions. Candidates undergo cognitive assessments and interviews, primarily focusing on literacy, language proficiency, and alignment with industry-specific educational backgrounds, such as finance for banking or engineering for aviation.

After selection, candidates participate in a generic training program tailored to the industry and company, followed by placement in entry-level positions across the organisation. Unfortunately, these placements are seldom aligned with the individual's personal preferences or strengths. This practice often serves the purpose of meeting nationalisation quotas, emphasising quantity over quality. Consequently, it can prove costly and restrictive for organisations attempting to pivot and reskill their workforce for future digital roles.

Specialist roles

After spending a few years honing their skills, employees often reach a stage of mastery in specialised functions like marketing, finance, or procurement officers. However, these roles are highly susceptible to automation, AI, and other emerging technologies if they remain repetitive in the nature of the day-to-day skills required to fulfil the mandates of the role.

Managerial roles

As employees excel in their roles, they may transition into managerial positions. Organisational investment typically involves developing the employee's ability to manage other employees, teams, and budgets, along with instilling organisational values and principles. At this stage, employees often hunger for growth, exposure, and development opportunities to advance to senior management. If these aspirations are not met, employees may become disengaged and seek employment elsewhere to further their careers.

Senior management

Reaching the senior management level requires a focus on career pathways and leadership exposure to retain top talent. Unfortunately, many organisations neglect to invest in the digital upskilling of their senior managers, despite their potential as future leaders. Current HR practices tend to focus on grooming high performers as successors within their respective functions or subject matters of expertise, overlooking the importance of targeted digital literacy. High attrition rates among national senior managers are often linked to feelings of undervaluation, limited career progression prospects, or a lack of exposure to organisational leadership.

Additionally, a significant challenge faced by most nationals at this level is the lack of knowledge sharing by their managers, leaving them unprepared for their next career phase. This challenge is often intentional, as managers seek to secure their long-term positions within the organisation.

Leadership

Organisations typically allocate resources for leadership development, primarily to meet nationalisation quotas. However, the challenge at this level lies in retaining national leaders, often accomplished through Long-Term Incentive Plans (LTIPs) where financial incentives are provided over several years in exchange for employee retention. While this may help retain leaders financially, it doesn't always equip them with a thorough understanding of digitisation's impact on their functions.

In summary, traditional human capital development structures have shown limitations in bridging the gap between nationalisation and digital transformation. To navigate this intersection successfully, organisations must reimagine their workforce development strategies, placing a stronger emphasis on aligning nationalisation goals with the rapidly evolving digital landscape.

CHAPTER 6

STRATEGIC FRAMEWORK

Future-Proof Human Capital Development

In the rapidly evolving landscape of business, characterized by the convergence of nationalisation goals and the imperative need for digital competence, traditional human capital development structures no longer suffice. Traditional approaches that have focused primarily on compliance with nationalisation quotas and the development of linear and siloed functional expertise are no longer sufficient to meet the demands of the digital age.

To navigate the challenges at the intersection of nationalisation and digital skills acquisition effectively, organisations must reimagine their approaches to talent cultivation and workforce development. To address this, organisations must embark on a transformative journey to future-proof their talent practices and human capital development strategies. This entails offering a comprehensive perspective on reshaping workforce strategies to not only meet the demands of the digital age but also simultaneously advance nationalisation objectives. In doing so, they can navigate this complex intersection and thrive in the ever-evolving business landscape.

The imperative for change

The existing human capital development model in many GCC countries, and indeed in many organisations globally, is often designed to meet immediate workforce needs. Typically, nationals are recruited in bulk through graduate programs or entry-level positions, trained for specific roles, and then progress along linear career paths. This conventional model, while serving the purpose of filling positions, is ill-suited for the dynamic demands of the digital era. To remain competitive and fulfil nationalisation goals, organisations must rethink their approach.

Key challenges of traditional human capital development

Traditional human capital structures face several critical challenges:

- Inflexibility: The rigid structure of traditional development pathways limits the adaptability of the workforce. It doesn't account for the rapid shifts in skill requirements brought about by digitalisation.
- Skill gaps: Nationals may find themselves trapped in roles that may become automated or less relevant due

to technological advancements. Skill development may not align with future job demands, and definitely not at the pace of technological advances and business requirements.

- Engagement and attrition: Employees can become disengaged and frustrated when their career progression stalls, leading to higher attrition rates. This attrition not only impacts organisational stability but also represents a loss of valuable talent.
- Lack of digital literacy: Traditional pathways often lack a focus on digital literacy and future-focused skills, leaving employees ill-prepared to navigate the digital landscape.

Principles of future-proof human capital development

Future-proof human capital development represents a paradigm shift in talent cultivation. It embodies a forward-looking, agile, and strategic approach to workforce development. Key principles include:

- Lifelong learning: Recognising that learning is a continuous journey, organisations must foster a culture of lifelong learning. It's not just about acquiring skills but also adapting to changing skill demands over time.
- Personalised development: Employees should have opportunities to personalise their development journeys based on their strengths, interests, and future career aspirations.

This approach enables individuals to align their skillsets with their digital ambitions.

- Digital integration: Digital literacy should be integrated into every level of the organisation. It's not limited to specific roles but permeates the entire workforce, from entry-level employees to senior leaders.
- Agility and adaptability: The ability to pivot and adapt to emerging technologies and trends should be embedded in development programs. This ensures that employees can respond effectively to changing market dynamics.
- Cross-functional exposure: Providing employees with cross-functional exposure and experiences can broaden their skillsets and make them more versatile. This is particularly valuable in a digital environment where interdisciplinary skills are increasingly essential.

FUTURE-PROOFING HUMAN CAPITAL DEVELOPMENT

The following framework outlines a future-proof human capital development structure for organisations in the GCC.

FIGURE 4.

Organizational Strategy

An agile, adaptive, and forward-thinking organisation that is in tune with the rapid shifts of the digital age and the complexities of nationalisation.

Unified vision:

Culture

- Continuous Learning Culture
- Collaboration & Inclusion
- Innovation & Agility
- Employee Feedback Loops

Competencies

- Environmental Scan: Forecasting Changes in Industry, Consumer Behaviour, Competitors, and Emerging Technologies.
- Technology Roadmap
- Gap Analysis & Competency Framework

Compliance

- Values-Based Policies
- Ethical Leadership
- Nationalization Strategy Shift: Quality vs Quantity
- Employee Experience

Talent & Skills Acquisition

Skills

	Skills Audit	Skills Gaps
	Skills Repository	Assess Transferable Skills

Hiring

Hire for Mindset, Learning Agility and Adaptability	Short- & Long-Term Digital Skills & STEM Talent Acquisition	
Competency-Based Succession Hiring	Place Nationals based on Strengths & Interests	

Adaptive Workforce Planning

Remote & Hybrid Work	Scenario Planning & Diversified Talent Pipeline Development	
Nationalisation Heat Mapping & Gap Analysis	Resource Planning	

Data & Analytics

- Data-Driven Insights and Forecasting
- Data Classification of Organisational Jobs & Skills
- Predictive and Adaptive Analytics
- Market and Career Intelligence

Talent Development

Leadership

Transformational Leadership	Collaborative Leadership	
Incentivize Knowledge Transfer	Digital & Tech Leadership Development	

Reskilling & Upskilling

Coaching & Mentoring	Technical Skills Development Partners	
Career Profiling & Mobility	On-The-Job Training based Apprenticeships	

Learning & Development

Application-Based Training	Personalised Learning Paths & Learning Communities	
Multi-Strategy Learning & Development Strategies	Cross-Functional Training	

Talent Management

Organisation Design & Reward

Simplify & Standardize Role Structures	Collaborative Leadership	
Cross-Functional Organisation Structure	Reward High Performers & De-emphasie Seniority	

Job Transition & Transformation

Redefinition of Disrupted Jobs	Human - Machine Division of Labor & Collaboration	
Role Transition Support	Career Pathways	

Performance & Knowledge Management

Knowledge Audits & Institutional Memory	Agile Goal Setting & Measuring Impact	
Contribution-Based Performance Measures	Learning and Reskilling Based KPIs	

External Partnerships

- Localized, Bespoke & Diverse Digital Education & Training
- Digital Academies & Digital Learning Platforms
- Fostering an Innovation Ecosystem and Hubs
- Public-Private Partnerships: Joint Ventures for Skills Exchange

To transition from a traditional to a future-proof human capital development model, organisations must firstly acknowledge a paradigm shift in the social contracts with their employees. AT&T, the largest telecommunications company in the United States, best described this new social contract between the organisation and its employees in this way:

> *'You can be a lifelong employee if you are ready to be a lifelong learner. We will give you the platform but you have to opt in ... you can be anything you want in this system. But again, you have to opt in. The executive's role here is to define the vision for the future. The company's responsibility is to provide the tools and platform for employees to get there, and the individual's role is to provide the selection and motivation. We need to make sure that anyone who leaves here [does not do so] because we did not provide them the platform – that it was their lack of motivation that did not make it happen.'* (Harvard Business School)

With this new social contract between employees and the organisation, we begin an exploration into the paradigm shift that traditional HR functions must undergo to future-proof human capital development in the digital age.

Organisational strategy

- Definition: Organisational strategy is a comprehensive plan that outlines an organisation's vision, goals, and the methods to achieve these objectives. It involves aligning resources and actions with the mission, vision, and values of the organisation.

- Relevance: Organisational strategy is relevant because it provides the north star of the organisation's ambitions, such as entering new markets and customer acquisition ambitions, and this provides the strategic direction for the organisation to navigate complex challenges, like integrating nationalisation objectives with digital advancement in the context of its overall direction and strategy, ensuring agility, adaptability, and foresight in decision-making.

- Unified vision: To effectively address the intersecting challenges of nationalisation objectives and the looming digital skills deficit, organisations must foster a unified vision. This vision should encapsulate agility, adaptability, and foresight, allowing entities to nimbly adjust to the ever-accelerating digital shifts. Crucially, for organisations within the GCC, intertwining nationalisation priorities within their talent cultivation practices of the future is paramount. This ensures that as they propel forward in the realm of digital innovation, they concurrently champion and embed nationalisation at the core of their progress.

Culture

- Definition: Organisational culture refers to the collective values, beliefs, and principles of organisational members, which shape their behaviours and practices.

- Relevance: Culture is crucial as it influences all aspects of an organisation, from employee engagement and performance to innovation and adaptability. A culture fostering continuous learning, collaboration, inclusion, and agility ensures an organisation thrives in a dynamic digital era.

Culture

- Continuous learning culture: The digital era thrives on swift transformations. For companies to stay at the forefront, embedding continuous learning as a foundational principle is essential. This means consistently revitalising training initiatives and equipping employees with tools to enhance their competencies. Equally vital is nurturing a growth mindset among employees, fostering an intrinsic drive for self-improvement.
- Collaboration and inclusion: Diverse teams yield multi-faceted insights. To fully harness this potential, organisations must dismantle silos, facilitating seamless collaboration across teams and functions. Cultivating a culture that emphasises both collaboration and inclusion ensures comprehensive problem-solving and guarantees every voice is not only heard but cherished. Celebrating diversity and actively fostering inclusion further strengthens this dynamic, ensuring a richer, more holistic organisational perspective.
- Innovation and agility: In today's fast-paced digital age, stagnation is a significant impediment to growth. To thrive, organisations must instil a culture that not only champions novel ideas but also accelerates their realisation.

Embracing innovation requires a conducive environment where risk-taking is rewarded, diverse perspectives are sought, and a relentless pursuit of improvement is ingrained in the organisational ethos. Meanwhile, agility goes beyond mere adaptability; it signifies an organisation's proactive readiness to pivot and reshape strategies in response to the dynamic digital milieu. Together, innovation and agility form the bedrock for a future-resilient organisation – one that can envision, evolve, and excel amid constant change.

- Employee feedback loops: Ground-level insights are often the most illuminating. By establishing robust two-way communication channels, such as the 'voice of the employee' feedback loops, organisations can capture real-time sentiments, concerns, and suggestions. This regular and meaningful engagement not only offers a clear view into the efficacy of existing strategies but also highlights opportunities for refinement. Actively seeking, listening to, and acting upon employee feedback fosters a culture of transparency, collaboration, and continuous improvement, positioning the organisation for long-term success.

Competencies

- Definition: Organisational competencies are the combination of skills, knowledge, and behaviours that are critical in enabling an organisation to achieve its strategic goals.

- Relevance: Competencies are vital for maintaining competitive advantage as they help organisations adapt to industry trends, technological evolutions, and changing market demands. By identifying and cultivating necessary competencies, organisations ensure sustained relevance and growth.

Competencies

- Environmental scan: Constant vigilance of industry trends, consumer inclinations, competitor actions, and burgeoning technological evolutions is crucial. By proactively immersing themselves in this ever-shifting landscape, organisations can better identify and cultivate the competencies needed for sustained relevance. This not only ensures that strategies are dynamic and adaptive but also reinforces an ethos of continuous growth and improvement within the organisation.
- Technology roadmap: Charting the digital horizon necessitates a lucid technology roadmap. This requires assessing current capabilities, projecting future technological demands, and crafting a strategy to address the disparities. Critically, aligning this roadmap with the necessary organisational competencies ensures not only the adoption of new technologies but also the seamless integration of these tools into the core operational fabric, driving sustainable progress and innovation.
- Gap analysis and competency framework: Drawing from the in-depth knowledge acquired through environmental scanning and the strategic guidance of the

technology roadmap, it's vital to assess the present skills and competencies within the organisation and compare them to forecasted future needs. This comparison identifies specific skill and competency shortfalls. Grounded in this thorough analysis, organisations can craft informed training programs and fine-tune hiring strategies, ensuring they remain adaptable, skilled, and forward-thinking.

Compliance

- Definition: Compliance in an organisation refers to adhering to laws, regulations, guidelines, and specifications relevant to its business processes.
- Relevance: Compliance is essential for legal and ethical functioning, building trust with stakeholders, and avoiding legal penalties. Compliance ensures organisations operate responsibly, maintain integrity, and align with national and international standards, including those related to digital transformation and nationalisation goals.

Compliance

- Values-based policies: In a world where businesses are increasingly held to higher ethical and moral standards, it's essential for organisations to ground their policies in core values. Such policies, rooted in integrity and transparency, not only ensure adherence to regulatory mandates but also foster trust both internally among employees and externally with stakeholders.

- Ethical leadership: True compliance and organisational integrity starts at the helm. Leaders must not only exemplify a commitment to ethical practices and the core values of the organisation but also champion its strategic direction and digital adoption. It's imperative for leaders to live and breathe the changes the organisation aims for, from moral integrity to the responsible and transparent use of technologies and data to demonstrating continuous learning first. When they align actions and decisions with these guiding principles, a clear precedent is set for the entire workforce, cultivating a culture of trust, accountability, and forward momentum.

- Nationalisation strategy shift – quality vs. quantity: The focus of nationalisation should transition from merely meeting numeric quotas to emphasising the quality of roles and opportunities offered to nationals. By prioritising meaningful engagement and value-driven roles for nationals, organisations not only comply with mandates but also enrich the talent pool, fostering genuine growth and development within the workforce.

- Employee experience: Compliance isn't just about rules and regulations, it's intrinsically linked to the experience of employees. A positive, respectful, and inclusive work environment ensures adherence to both the letter and the spirit of compliance mandates. By emphasising the wellbeing, growth, and satisfaction of employees, organisations mitigate risks and cultivate a thriving, engaged workforce.

Talent and skills acquisition

The very core of future-proofing an organisation lies in its talent acquisition strategy.

Skills

- Skills audit:
  - Importance: An audit of organisational skills serves as the bedrock for future planning. By understanding where the organisation currently stands, leadership can make informed decisions about the path forward.
  - Relation to organisational competencies: Mapping current skills against identified organisational competencies reveals where the workforce is strong and where development is needed. This crucial analysis sets the stage for subsequent human capital development interventions.

- Skills repository:
  - Significance: A centralised skills repository streamlines talent management, serving as a 'knowledge bank' of employee skills.
  - Support to reskilling and upskilling: With a clear view of employees' proficiencies, it's easier to match them with tailored training programs, ensuring they remain at the cutting edge of their roles as well as the future skills required by the organisation.
  - Succession planning: A comprehensive skills repository aids in identifying potential leaders within the

organisation, making succession planning more strategic and informed.
- Career transition: By understanding each employee's strengths, organisations can guide career development paths, ensuring employees evolve with the changing needs of the business.

- Skills gaps:
  - Critical role: Pinpointing the skills gaps is instrumental in directing the learning and development strategies of an organisation.
  - Closing the digital skills gap: Recognising these gaps, especially in the realm of digital skills, helps organisations prioritise training initiatives, ensuring they are equipped to thrive in an increasingly digital landscape. By understanding both short-term and long-term needs, organisations can deploy targeted strategies that address immediate concerns while also building a foundation for the future.

- Transferable skills:
  - Significance: As the digital age progresses, certain roles may become obsolete, but the skills employees possess can often be redirected based on the transferable skills they have amassed throughout their career and retraining for capability gaps.
  - Pivoting in disrupted roles: Identifying and categorising employees' transferable skills ensures that, even if a particular role is disrupted by technology, the expertise of those employees isn't lost. Instead, they can be

transitioned into new roles where their skills can shine in a different context, promoting organisational agility and resilience in the face of change.

Hiring

Hire for mindset, learning agility, and adaptability in the face of digital disruption.

Importance in a rapidly changing landscape

- Digital disruption: The accelerating pace of technological innovation means that jobs will face numerous disruptions in the coming years. As roles evolve, some may become obsolete while others may undergo significant transformations.
- The need for adaptability: In such a fluid environment, hiring for specific technical skills alone isn't enough. The agility to adapt, underpinned by the right mindset, is a paramount attribute. Individuals with learning agility will be better equipped to navigate these shifts, ensuring they can learn, unlearn, and relearn as per the organisation's evolving needs and the broader digital landscape.

Long-term benefits in a digital era

- Sustained relevance: Employees with a growth mindset are not only proactive learners but also resilient in the face of change. Their capacity to adapt ensures they remain relevant, regardless of how their specific roles evolve due to digital disruptions.

- Alignment with organisational evolution: As organisations undergo digital transformations, employees who are agile learners will be at the forefront, aligning themselves with organisational goals, embracing new technologies, and consistently making efforts to upskill. Their adaptability will be instrumental in ensuring both individual and organisational success in a digitally driven future.

Short-term and long-term digital skills and STEM talent acquisition amid the digital revolution

Imperative needs in a digital era

- Technological integration: As technological advancements become the backbone of business operations, the imperative to acquire talent with proficient digital skills and science, technology, engineering and mathematics (STEM) backgrounds becomes undeniable.
- Increasing STEM recruitment: To benchmark organisational tech competence, a significant uptick in STEM recruitment will become a pivotal key performance indicator (KPI). This recruitment drive encompasses sourcing from both the external market and internally from employees who've undergone reskilling programs.

Revamping talent acquisition strategies

- Tapping into the gig economy: Given the dynamic nature of technological needs, organisations should leverage the gig economy, drawing on a flexible workforce for specialised, short-term projects.
- Hiring specialists from the tech industry: As a short-term strategy, bringing in seasoned professionals from the tech domain, such as data scientists, can provide immediate expertise. These experts can then function as catalysts, accelerating the organisation's digital transformation journey.
- Supporting external experts with nationals: While hiring external talent provides immediate competency, pairing them with national employees in training ensures a sustainable transfer of knowledge. For instance, an externally hired data scientist can mentor and guide a national data scientist in training, fostering a long-term internal talent pipeline.

Internal competency development

- Sustainable long-term strategy: While short-term talent acquisition addresses immediate needs, organisations must also focus on the long-term horizon. This involves substantial investments in reskilling and upskilling initiatives, preparing the internal workforce for the technological demands of the future.
- Increasing internal STEM capacities: By transforming current employees into STEM experts through targeted

training programs, organisations not only retain institutional knowledge but also ensure a sustainable, future-ready talent base.

Future-proofing and organisational competitiveness

- Harnessing the power of emerging technologies: With a robust blend of short-term and long-term talent strategies, organisations position themselves optimally to exploit emerging technologies, from AI to blockchain and beyond.
- Sustainability and competitive edge: By ensuring a steady influx of digital and STEM talent, organisations guarantee their resilience, adaptability, and competitive edge in a market increasingly dictated by technological prowess.

Strategic placement of nationals: Strengths, interests, and technological aspirations

Internal development and placement

- Recognising strengths: Identify and nurture the innate capabilities of current national employees, aligning them with roles that will maximise their contributions and job satisfaction.
- Career pathways: Offer clear trajectories that align with their evolving strengths and interests, ensuring they envision a long-term future within the organisation.
- Continuous alignment: Regular reviews and feedback sessions keep career paths and roles relevant, addressing any shifts in interests or capabilities over time.

External acquisition and integration

- Tech career visibility: For potential national hires, provide clear insights into available tech roles and their significance. Use information sessions, workshops, and mentorship programs to clarify the potential and nuances of tech careers within the organisation.
- Strategic attraction: Tailor recruitment campaigns to resonate with the aspirations and interests of nationals, emphasising the opportunities for growth, innovation, and impact.
- Role alignment: During the hiring process, ensure that nationals are matched with positions that not only fulfil organisational needs but also align closely with their personal strengths and aspirations, fostering engagement and retention from the outset.

Aligning hiring practices with competency gaps for long-term succession

Strategic foresight

- Anticipating future needs: To ensure the long-term viability and leadership continuity of an organisation, it's imperative to align hiring strategies with anticipated competency gaps. As the digital landscape evolves, so do the competencies required to lead and drive innovation within critical roles.

Tailored recruitment

- Targeted talent acquisition: Instead of generic hiring, organisations should hone their recruitment efforts towards candidates who can fill identified competency voids, particularly in leadership and crucial digital positions. This means emphasising not just immediate skills, but potential for growth and adaptability.

Integration with succession planning

- Proactive development: Once identified and onboarded, these hires should be integrated into a tailored development program, ensuring that they are primed for succession into leadership or vital digital roles. This isn't just about immediate role readiness, but about sculpting the future leaders and innovators of the organisation.

Benefits

- Sustainability and growth: Such a strategic approach to hiring ensures the organisation remains resilient, future-proofed, and poised for growth. By planning for the long term, firms can secure their position in the vanguard of their industry, adeptly navigating the digital future.
- Optimised ROI: Investing in talent that fills competency gaps means resources are channelled effectively, leading to greater ROI in terms of employee performance, innovation, and leadership continuity.

By ensuring that hiring practices are intertwined with identified competency gaps, organisations can proactively shape their future, ensuring that they are not just reactive to changes, but are strategically poised to leverage them.

Adaptive workforce planning in the face of digital disruption

Remote and hybrid work

- Significance: With the rise of the digital age and the global shift towards remote and hybrid work arrangements, the very nature of organisational operation is undergoing transformation.
- Flexibility and access: These modern work structures offer flexibility, enhance morale and productivity, and broaden the organisation's talent reach, enabling them to onboard diverse expertise irrespective of geographical constraints.

Scenario planning and diversified talent pipeline development

- Digital readiness: As new technologies permeate business operations, it's paramount for organisations to pre-emptively plan for various digital disruption scenarios. This foresight ensures resilience and adaptability amid tech-driven changes.
- Strategic foresight: A diversified talent pipeline is essential to meet the demands of these impending disruptions. By nurturing a talent mix equipped with diverse skills and perspectives, organisations set themselves up to adeptly

navigate varied challenges and harness the benefits of digital innovations.

Nationalisation heat mapping and gap analysis

- Holistic view: Understanding the current concentration of the national workforce across various levels and divisions is pivotal. This comprehensive view aids in assessing whether the distribution aligns with future organisational competencies.
- Strategic realignment: With insights from the analysis, organisations can strategically reallocate and recruit national talent. This ensures compliance with nationalisation goals and places nationals in roles where they can meaningfully contribute and evolve in tandem with the organisation's future trajectory.

Resource planning
with a focus on diversified talent

- Optimisation goal: Efficient and strategic allocation of human capital is crucial. This not only addresses current needs but ensures that talent aligns with future technological integrations and organisational shifts.
- Incorporating diverse talent streams: Effective resource planning integrates the diversified talent pipeline, ensuring that the organisation has the human resources who are equipped to harness emerging technologies and methodologies, keeping them at the forefront of their industry.

Talent development in the age of digital disruption

As technological shifts redefine industries, fostering a future-ready workforce becomes paramount. Below is a refined strategy to navigate this transformative era.

Leadership in the digital age

Transformational leadership

- Visionary influence: Leaders must inspire employees, driving them to exceed their potential and align with the organisation's overarching vision in a tech-saturated landscape.

Collaborative leadership

- Cross-functional synergy: Leaders should champion collaboration across functions, de-emphasising seniority to prioritise merit and ability. This fosters a dynamic environment where organisational goals are pursued holistically, leveraging diverse skillsets and perspectives across departments.

Knowledge transfer

- Incentives for shared wisdom: Encouraging the dissemination of essential knowledge through rewards, such as bonuses linked to in-depth 360° feedback, motivates seasoned leaders and key digital talents to mentor and guide the next wave of professionals. For instance, offering additional compensation to those who excel in coaching and supporting the integration of national successors can further enhance this process.

Digital proficiency for leaders and technical talent

- Strategic tech acumen for leaders: Modern leaders must have a robust understanding of how technology drives innovation, fosters competitive advantage, and ensures customer-centricity. While not necessarily experts in the technicalities, they should be adept at leveraging technology strategically to achieve organisational objectives.
- Continuous technical learning for digital talent: Digital professionals should commit to ongoing technical learning to stay abreast of advancements and best practices. Their depth of technical expertise is pivotal for operationalising and maximising the potential of new technologies within the organisation.

Reskilling and upskilling for the digital age

Coaching and mentoring

- Digital knowledge dissemination: Harnessing the expertise of digital talents within the organisation can foster a culture of continuous learning, where these experts actively educate and mentor their peers on essential digital skills and insights.

- Transition support: As roles evolve with technological advancements, role transition coaches become indispensable. They provide tailored guidance to employees, ensuring a smoother adaptation to new roles and responsibilities after upskilling.

Career profiling and mobility

- Data-driven career mapping: Using data and analytics to understand employees' existing transferable skills can provide invaluable insights. This information can be leveraged to offer alternative roles and pathways, ensuring employees have opportunities to transition seamlessly when faced with job disruptions.
- Empowering transitions: Offering clear alternative career paths based on these insights ensures that employees remain engaged and motivated, even as the work landscape shifts.

On-the-job training and apprenticeships

- Practical skill development: These initiatives ensure that employees are both knowledgeable and possess the practical skills required to navigate real-world challenges. Direct on-the-job experience solidifies learning and ensures that the newly acquired skills are directly applicable to the workplace.

Technical skill development partnerships

- Cross-industry collaboration: Building relationships with industry stakeholders and academic entities ensures that the organisation's technical training remains current and aligned with emerging digital trends. Such partnerships also ensure a diverse and well-rounded approach to technical skill development, placing the organisation at the forefront of digital readiness.

Holistic learning and development for the modern workforce

Application-based training

- Immediate utility:
  - Accelerated skill acquisition: Directly linking training to real-world tasks reduces the time needed for employees to become proficient in new skills. This swift approach to upskilling is instrumental in quickly addressing the digital skills gap.
  - Immediate competency: Employees don't just learn; they immediately become competent in tasks that directly impact their roles, boosting their productivity and confidence.

- Experiential learning:
  - Practical engagement: Leveraging scenarios and simulations empowers employees to practise and refine their skills in a controlled environment, ensuring they are job-ready faster.
  - Bridging knowledge to action: Such experiential methods effectively connect theoretical knowledge to tangible outcomes, enhancing both understanding

and application, which subsequently reduces the transition time from learning to implementation.

Multi-strategy learning and development (L&D) approaches

- Diverse techniques, holistic learning:
  - Varied learning platforms: Incorporating open learning digital academies, application-based training sessions, specialised technical programs, and professional education ensures a rich and diverse learning ecosystem.
  - Catering to every learner: With an array of modalities, from traditional classroom sessions to e-learning modules, organisations can address the unique learning needs of every individual, thereby ensuring that no employee is left behind in the digital transformation journey.

Adaptive L&D

- Continuous evolution: As the digital landscape rapidly evolves, it's crucial to keep L&D strategies fresh and updated. Feedback-driven and dynamic learning approaches ensure that training interventions remain aligned with both organisational goals and individual needs.

Cross-functional training

- Integrated business perspective:
  - Breaking down barriers: Cross-functional training actively dismantles organisational silos, promoting

seamless collaboration and knowledge sharing across departments.
- Cultivating innovation: By understanding and appreciating the intricacies of various functions, employees can make connections that lead to innovative solutions and practices.

- Facilitating organisational synergy:
  - Promoting a learning culture: A workforce familiar with multiple facets of the organisation is more adaptable and capable of pivoting into new roles, thus contributing to a resilient and agile enterprise. Such an environment fosters continuous learning and adaptability, foundational pillars for future success in the digital age.

TALENT MANAGEMENT

Harnessing the full potential of your workforce is pivotal for long-term organisational success.

Organisation design and rewards

Strategic succession planning
- Inclusive continuity: While leadership transitions remain pivotal, it's equally crucial to ensure succession for vital

digital roles. Effective retention plans and thorough knowledge exposure for successors are imperative to guarantee business continuity, especially in the face of unforeseen attrition.

Meritocratic rewards

- Rewarding impact: While recognising high performers is key, it's also vital to emphasise rewards based on contribution-driven effort, transcending traditional seniority. This approach fosters an environment where true value addition is appreciated and incentivised across all organisational levels.

Cross-functional collaboration

- Digital synergy: As digital development inherently necessitates multidisciplinary inputs, fostering a culture of collaboration becomes paramount. Reducing bureaucratic barriers and promoting free interdepartmental interactions will be central to achieving swift and innovative digital solutions.

Streamlined roles and structures

- Alignment with purpose: Beyond simplifying job roles for operational clarity, it's vital to ensure that these roles are strategically aligned with overarching organisational goals, driving each individual's efforts towards a shared vision of success.

Job transition and transformation

Pathway clarity

- Resilient trajectories: In the face of digital disruption, crafting well-articulated career paths for every role is paramount. This equips employees for potential reskilling and transitions and instils confidence by outlining a comprehensive view of their evolving career journey within the organisation.

Transition aid

- Guided adaptation: Incorporating career transition coaches is essential as they provide holistic support, linking employees to clear reskilling timelines and post-reskilling journey discussions. This ensures a structured and supportive transition, minimising anxieties and optimising outcomes.

Digital relevance

- Proactive evolution: With technology's swift advancements, it's imperative to forecast the incline and decline of roles impacted by imminent digital shifts. By proactively identifying these changes, organisations can stay ahead, ensuring staff and roles remain relevant and primed for the future.

Human—machine synergy

- Optimised collaboration: Strategically dividing tasks between humans and technology maximises operational efficiency. By deploying technology for repetitive and low-value tasks, human resources can be channelled into roles requiring decision-making, management, and creative nuances, enhancing overall organisational effectiveness.

Performance and knowledge management

Preserving organisational wisdom

- Dynamic knowledge retention: By regularly conducting knowledge audits, organisations can identify and fill knowledge gaps while preserving the essential wisdom that forms their foundation. These audits also facilitate smoother transitions, ensuring that valuable insights and expertise aren't lost but are instead transferred and built upon.

Value-based performance

- Meritocratic culture: Moving beyond traditional metrics and embracing contribution-based performance evaluations ensures that genuine effort and tangible outcomes are recognised. This approach not only rewards employees who drive results but also cultivates a culture where impactful contributions are at the forefront.

Growth-driven KPIs

- Adaptive skill metrics: In an era where skills become obsolete rapidly due to technological advancements, KPIs should mirror this dynamism. By incorporating learning and reskilling metrics, organisations demonstrate their commitment to employee growth, ensuring their talent pool remains contemporary and competitive.

Agile objectives

- Fluid goal setting: In a constantly evolving digital landscape, organisational goals must be adaptable. Implementing agile methodologies in setting and reviewing objectives ensures that targets are relevant to current challenges. Moreover, using data-driven techniques to measure goal attainment with exactness ensures accurate reflections of progress and areas of improvement.

Data and analytics

- Anticipatory insights: Leveraging data-driven forecasting to foresee trends and adapt proactively.
- Efficient resource mapping: Using data to classify and allocate jobs and skills optimally.
- Alignment with market dynamics: Consistently updating strategies based on market and career intelligence.
- Proactive decision-making: Employing predictive and adaptive analytics for informed, forward-looking choices.

External partnerships

- Relevant digital learning: Engaging in region-specific, tailor-made, and diversified digital training guarantees relevance and impact.
- Edge through collaboration: Forming alliances with digital academies and learning platforms offers state-of-the-art resources and techniques.
- Bridging the gap: Public–private collaborations, especially skills exchange joint ventures, can significantly narrow skill and nationalisation deficits.

- Innovation culture: Cultivating hubs and ecosystems that foster innovation ensures an organisation stays ahead in the evolving digital landscape.

By comprehensively adopting this framework, organisations can not only adeptly manage the intricacies of nationalisation and digital transformation but also flourish within them.

Future-proof human capital development is not just a strategy, it's a necessity for organisations seeking to thrive in the digital age while fulfilling nationalisation objectives. It's a holistic approach that places continuous learning, adaptability, and digital literacy at its core. By reimagining talent cultivation in this manner, organisations can harness the potential of their workforce, foster innovation, and contribute to both their own success and the broader societal progress envisioned through nationalisation efforts. This chapter sets the stage for a transformative journey toward a future-proofed workforce, where individuals are equipped not only to meet the demands of today but to shape the opportunities of tomorrow.

As we conclude our exploration in this chapter of the delicate interplay between nationalisation and the growing need for digital proficiency, we prepare to embark on a journey through the vast landscape of cutting-edge technologies in Chapter 7. This chapter is designed to introduce you to these pivotal technologies, then contextualise them within the framework of the GCC's nationalisation and digital skills objectives.

ESSENTIAL TECHNOLOGIES AND CAPABILITIES

Pioneering the Digital Frontier

Welcome to our exploration into the dynamic digital terrain that is reshaping business landscapes across the GCC. In this chapter, we embark on a profound journey into pivotal technological innovations, each poised to reshape industries and ignite transformative shifts. Our mission is to empower GCC organisations with a profound understanding of these essential technologies, revealing their vast potential within the regional context and the skills and roles primed for success in this digital ecosystem. Throughout these pages, we unveil not only the transformative capabilities of these technologies but also underscore the crucial skillsets required to harness their power, guiding readers toward adaptable roles that will ensure the GCC's prominence in the ongoing digital revolution.

CORE TECHNOLOGIES

In the ever-evolving digital landscape, certain core technologies form the backbone of modern business operations. These technologies are foundational, shaping the way organisations function, interact, and innovate. In this section, we explore some of these core technologies, their relevance in the GCC region, the essential skills required to work with them, and existing roles that can upskill to harness their potential.

Cloud computing

Introduction: At its essence, cloud computing offers on-demand computing resources, from applications to storage centres, without the user needing to own or maintain physical infrastructure.

Benefits in the GCC: Cloud computing offers scalability and cost-efficiency, crucial for the GCC's burgeoning startup scene. For larger enterprises, it provides agility, enabling rapid adaptation to market changes.

Deployment models

- Public cloud: Services offered over the public internet, suitable for various business needs and scalable to any extent.
- Private cloud: Dedicated services for individual enterprises, offering enhanced security and customisation.

- Hybrid cloud: Combines public and private, giving businesses flexibility and more deployment options.

Service models

- IaaS (infrastructure as a service): Provides users with internet-based access to storage and computing power.
- PaaS (platform as a service): Offers a platform allowing customers to develop, run, and manage applications without dealing with infrastructure complexities.
- SaaS (software as a service): Delivers software over the internet, eliminating the need for local installations or running applications on individual computers.

Challenges and considerations for organisations: Discussing concerns like data security and compliance with local regulations and ensuring uninterrupted services. Addressing the importance of choosing the right service providers, understanding service-level agreements, and ensuring redundancy and disaster recovery capabilities.

Skills required

Professionals working with cloud computing should possess the following skills:

- Cloud platforms: Familiarity with major cloud platforms like AWS, Azure, or Google Cloud.
- Infrastructure as code (IAC): Knowledge of IAC tools like Terraform and CloudFormation.
- Security: Expertise in cloud security practices and compliance.

- Containers and orchestration: Understanding of containerisation tools like Docker and Kubernetes.
- Serverless computing: Proficiency in serverless architecture and functions.

Existing roles for upskilling

- System administrators: Can transition to cloud administrators.
- Developers: Can upskill to become cloud-native application developers.
- Network engineers: Can specialise in cloud networking.
- Security professionals: Can focus on cloud security and compliance.

Data centres

Significance: As the physical embodiment of the cloud, data centres house the servers, storage devices, and networking equipment that power our digital world.

Role in the GCC: Highlighting the importance of local data centres to address data sovereignty concerns, reduce latency, and enhance service reliability.

Modern innovations

- Green data centres: As the GCC pushes towards sustainable initiatives, the concept of environmentally friendly data centres that minimise resource usage becomes paramount.

- Modular data centres: Offering scalability, these are pre-fabricated mobile structures that can be easily deployed and scaled as per requirements.
- Edge data centres: Located closer to end-users, they help in processing data nearer to the source, reducing latency and enhancing user experience.

Security and compliance: Emphasising the criticality of physical and digital security measures, from surveillance to cybersecurity protocols, ensuring data integrity and confidentiality.

Skillset evolution

Professionals involved with data centres should have the following skills:

- Data centre operations: Expertise in data centre management and maintenance.
- Virtualisation and hardware optimisation: Knowledge of virtualisation technologies to run and create virtual versions of systems. Enabling multiple virtual systems to run on a single physical system, therefore optimising hardware usage.
- Energy efficiency: Understanding of energy-efficient data centre practices.
- Data security: Skills in data security and compliance.
- Monitoring and analytics: Proficiency in data centre monitoring tools.

Upskilling opportunities
and career pathways for advancement

- Data centre technicians: Can advance to data centre administrators.
- Network administrators: Can specialise in data centre networking.
- Security analysts: Can focus on data centre security.

5G and beyond

Understanding 5G: The fifth generation of mobile network technology, 5G, is a leap forward, characterised by its remarkable speed, reliability, and capacity to simultaneously connect a multitude of devices. This advancement stands to redefine connectivity, pushing the boundaries of current capabilities.

The GCC perspective: In the GCC region, 5G's potential is vast, stretching from the development of smart cities to the expansion of the industrial IoT. This technology is poised to bolster connectivity across various sectors, promising to catalyse economic and technological growth.

Infrastructure imperatives: Transitioning to 5G necessitates a comprehensive overhaul of existing infrastructure. This includes the deployment of new antennas, the update of software systems, and fostering wider acceptance of the technology among device manufacturers and consumers alike.

Opportunities and hurdles: The advent of 5G offers unparalleled opportunities, promising speeds and connectivity that were previously unthinkable. However, the journey is not without its challenges. Addressing concerns such as the substantial investment required for setup and lingering health worries is imperative for the successful adoption of 5G.

Empowering the GCC: Mastery of 5G and its underlying technologies can secure the GCC a formidable position on the global stage. For organisations within the region, investing in and understanding these advancements is crucial not only for staying relevant today but also for future-proofing their operations.

Skillset evolution

- Wireless networking: Proficiency in the nuances of wireless communication protocols and technologies is essential.
- IoT integration: A deep understanding of IoT systems and their applications is crucial for harnessing the full potential of 5G.
- Network security: Ensuring the security of 5G and IoT networks is paramount and requires specialised knowledge and skills.
- Emerging technologies: Staying abreast of technologies on the horizon, such as 6G, and their possible impacts and applications is vital.

Upskilling opportunities and career pathways for advancement

- Network engineers: Professionals in this role can pivot to specialise in the deployment and management of 5G networks, setting the foundation for the next generation of connectivity.

- IoT specialists: These experts can broaden their scope to include 5G-enabled IoT solutions, leveraging the enhanced capabilities of 5G for innovative applications.
- Security professionals: With the advent of 5G, focusing on the unique security challenges it presents, especially in conjunction with IoT devices, becomes a crucial area of expertise.

These core technologies serve as the foundation for digital innovation and growth. Professionals in the GCC region have the opportunity to upskill and reskill, ensuring they are equipped to harness the potential of these technologies in their respective domains.

GENERATIVE TECHNOLOGIES

Definition: Generative technologies encompass systems that autonomously create new content, designs, or solutions based on patterns learnt from existing data. Primarily rooted in AI, particularly machine learning (ML) and deep learning (DL), these technologies have transformative potential.

Understanding generative technologies

- AI: Machines mimicking human intelligence processes, encompassing learning, reasoning, and self-correction.

- ML: An AI subset, ML allows machines to learn from data, predicting outcomes or recognising patterns without being explicitly programmed.
- DL: A subfield of ML, DL employs neural networks with many layers to analyse intricate patterns in vast datasets, fitting for tasks like image and voice recognition.

How they work: Generative technologies, akin to training an artist by showcasing myriad paintings until they craft their own, learn from vast datasets. They identify patterns, then use these patterns to generate new content. A standout model is the generative adversarial network (GAN) where two neural networks are trained in tandem. The generator creates fake data, and the discriminator differentiates it from real data. Over iterations, the generator's outputs become indistinguishable from real data.

Applications in the GCC

- Digital art and heritage preservation: Crafting digital art or simulating age-old designs, preserving the GCC's rich culture.
- Music and entertainment: Creating region-specific tracks or entertainment content.
- Urban planning: Auto-generating infrastructural designs in line with the region's climate and architectural aesthetics.
- Pharmaceuticals: Aiding regional pharma by suggesting potential drug compounds.
- Fashion: Innovating in the Middle Eastern fashion space with new designs or textiles.

Key considerations for GCC businesses

- Cultural resonance: Ensuring generated content aligns with regional sentiments and cultural norms.
- Investment in education: Nurturing local talent in AI and ML to lead innovation.
- Infrastructure: Upgrading digital infrastructure to support data-heavy tasks of generative tech.
- Regulation and ethics: Formulating guidelines to prevent misuse (e.g. deepfakes) and ensure responsible technology deployment.

Typical uses of AI in corporates

- Customer service: Chatbots and virtual assistants, driven by AI, are now common for handling customer queries, complaints, and feedback.
- Sales and marketing: AI tools can analyse vast amounts of data to predict consumer behaviour, enabling targeted marketing campaigns.
- Human resources: AI can assist in screening resumes, predicting candidate success, and even monitoring employee wellbeing.
- Finance: Automated fraud detection, investment predictions, and risk assessments are all facilitated by AI.
- Supply chain and logistics: AI can predict demand, optimise routes for delivery, and manage inventories in real time.
- Product recommendations: E-commerce giants use AI to recommend products to users based on browsing history, purchases, and search.

- Decision support: Executives use AI-driven insights to make informed decisions on product launches, expansions, and other major business moves.

The AI skills gap and the subsequent evolution of jobs

Generative technologies, while promising productivity boosts, also foreshadow job disruptions. Roles involving repetitive tasks or basic content creation may face redundancies. However, this also presents an opportunity. Instead of jobs of the past, the focus may shift to overseeing AI processes, refining outputs, or roles we haven't yet envisioned. For the GCC, where diversification away from oil is a strategic focus, generative technologies offer both challenges and opportunities for the job market. Investment in upskilling and continuous learning is pivotal to ride this wave.

In the AI, ML, and DL domains, there's a pronounced difference between the demand for expertise and the available supply of skilled professionals.

Reasons for the gap

- Rapid technology evolution: AI, particularly ML and DL, is advancing rapidly, making it challenging for academic institutions to keep up.
- Specialisation: AI isn't just one field. It spans natural language processing, computer vision, and robotics, among others, each requiring a deep understanding.

- Practical experience: While theoretical knowledge is crucial, hands-on experience, such as working on real-world projects, is in higher demand than the supply available.

Implications

- Increased salaries: High demand and low supply have driven up compensation for AI professionals.
- Dependence on a few: Many companies may end up depending on a small team or even a single individual, creating a potential vulnerability.

The evolution of jobs

- Automation of repetitive tasks: AI, especially ML, is adept at automating tasks that are repetitive and rules-based, leading to potential job losses in areas like data entry, basic customer service, and certain manual labour tasks.
- Creation of new jobs: While AI will displace some jobs, it will also create new ones. Roles like ML trainers, who refine AI model outputs, or roles such as AI safety engineers, AI ethics officers, and algorithm bias auditors, will emerge.
- Shift in nature of jobs: Even jobs that aren't replaced will see a shift in their nature. For instance, a doctor might use AI for diagnosis assistance but will still be essential for patient care and decision-making.

Skillset evolution for generative technology

Professionals engaged with generative technologies are poised to expand their expertise through a comprehensive skillset that includes:

- ML: Proficiency in ML algorithms and frameworks enriches problem-solving capabilities.
- Natural language processing (NLP): Mastering NLP techniques unlocks new avenues in communication technologies.
- Data science: Skills in data pre-processing, feature engineering, and model evaluation are critical for extracting actionable insights.
- Programming: Expertise in languages like Python and R allows for more robust software solutions.
- Ethical AI: A strong grasp of ethical considerations ensures responsible AI development.
- AI strategy: Aligning AI initiatives with business objectives fosters strategic growth.
- Project management: Effective management of AI projects ensures streamlined operations.
- Change management: Facilitating AI adoption within organisations drives technological transformation.

These skills provide a solid foundation for professionals in the GCC to leverage their existing knowledge in specific domains, such as healthcare or finance, enabling them to transition into AI with ease. This shift not only enhances their career trajectories but also enriches their professional roles with cutting-edge technology.

Essential expertise in
AI governance and compliance

Professionals committed to AI governance and compliance play a pivotal role in shaping the ethical landscape of artificial intelligence. They are equipped with a powerful toolkit:

- AI ethics: Professionals possess a profound understanding of ethical AI principles, ensuring that AI solutions enhance societal wellbeing while avoiding harm. Their expertise is crucial in maintaining the moral compass of AI developments.
- Data privacy: With an in-depth knowledge of data protection laws, these experts safeguard sensitive information, building trust and ensuring that AI systems uphold the highest standards of privacy and security.
- Regulatory compliance: Mastery over industry-specific regulations enables these professionals to guide AI projects towards compliance excellence. Their strategic insights are essential in navigating the complex regulatory environments, ensuring that innovations proceed without compromising legal or ethical standards.

This specialised knowledge is indispensable as organisations strive to responsibly harness the transformative power of AI, ensuring that these advancements are implemented with integrity and accountability. Such expertise not only protects organisations but also defines the future of ethical AI deployment.

Career pathways for advancement

Opportunities for upskilling

- Data analysts evolve into data scientists specialising in ML, turning data into strategic assets.
- Software developers transform into AI developers, pioneering new software landscapes.
- Business analysts pivot to AI-driven analytics, enhancing decision-making processes.
- Project managers excel in AI project management, leading innovative projects.
- Business consultants emerge as AI strategy consultants, guiding companies through digital transformation.
- Change management specialists champion AI adoption strategies, steering organisational change.

Opportunities for reskilling

- Medical professionals transition into AI-driven healthcare solutions, improving patient care with technology.
- Financial analysts specialise in AI-driven fraud detection, securing financial ecosystems.
- Marketing specialists adapt to AI-driven marketing strategies, crafting targeted campaigns.
- Legal professionals focus on AI and data privacy law, navigating the complexities of tech law.
- AI ethics officers ensure ethical AI practices within organisations, maintaining trust and integrity.
- Compliance specialists concentrate on AI regulatory compliance, safeguarding organisational interests.

Generative technologies are catalysing a new era of innovation and automation. This dynamic shift offers professionals across various industries in the GCC endless opportunities to upskill and reskill, enabling them to harness the transformative power of AI in their respective domains. With these advancements, the workforce is set to thrive in an increasingly digital landscape, filled with opportunities for growth and innovation.

DATA AS THE NEW OIL

In the 21st century, data has emerged as a new form of currency, sometimes even surpassing the value of tangible assets. This axiom, 'data is the new oil', underlines the significant role that data plays in driving innovation, personalisation, and decision-making in modern businesses. Just as the Middle East sits at the top of the world's most significant oil reserves, becoming a hub of wealth and power, the region now has the potential to harness the immense power of data to drive its next phase of growth and diversification.

The analogy explained

- Origins: Both oil and data are raw materials, extracted from their environments and refined to produce valuable commodities – be it gasoline or actionable insights.
- Transformation: Much like crude oil, raw data isn't valuable in its unprocessed state. It requires tools, techniques, and expertise to refine and convert into actionable insights.

- Economic impact: Just as oil powered the Industrial Revolution, data is the driving force behind the digital revolution. It's shaping industries, economies, and political landscapes.

The GCC's unique position

- Data generation: With a rapidly growing digital user base, increased smartphone penetration, and a strong push towards digitalisation, the GCC is generating vast amounts of data at an unprecedented rate.
- Government initiatives: Many governments in the region, notably the UAE and Saudi Arabia, are investing heavily in digital transformation, ensuring that data is collected, stored, and analysed efficiently.
- Cultural shift: The region's youth, who form a significant portion of the population, are digital natives. Their online behaviours, preferences, and consumption patterns offer a wealth of data that, if harnessed correctly, can provide a competitive advantage to businesses.

Challenges of harnessing data

- Privacy and regulation: As data becomes more valuable, there's an increasing emphasis on user privacy and data protection. Ensuring compliance with evolving regulations, like the European Union's General Data Protection Regulation (GDPR) or local equivalents, is crucial.
- Data storage and management: The sheer volume of data being generated requires advanced storage solutions, robust data management strategies, and efficient retrieval systems.

- Skills shortage: The region faces a shortage of data scientists and analysts. Building a skilled workforce capable of analysing and drawing insights from data is a pressing challenge.

Actionable steps for organisations to achieve data literacy

- Invest in data infrastructure: From cloud storage solutions to advanced data analytics tools, ensuring the right infrastructure is in place is the first step.
- Prioritise data literacy: All levels of the organisation, from entry-level employees to top executives, should possess a basic understanding of data and its potential impact.
- Collaborate and partner: Establish partnerships with universities, think tanks, and tech companies to stay abreast of the latest data technologies and methodologies.
- Ethical considerations: It's vital to use data responsibly, ensuring that personal information is protected, and biases are avoided in data analysis.

While oil has been central to the GCC's growth and prosperity in the 20th century, data promises to play a similar role in the 21st. The potential is immense, but realising it requires vision, strategy, and a commitment to innovation. For the leaders of the region, understanding and leveraging the power of data will be instrumental in leading their organisations into a prosperous future.

SKILLSET EVOLUTION
FOR DATA PROFESSIONALS

Professionals engaged in data-centric roles are at the fore-front of the digital transformation, equipped with a diverse and essential skillset:

- Data analytics: Mastery of data analysis tools and techniques that unveil actionable insights.
- Data visualisation: Proficient in translating complex data into clear, impactful visual narratives.
- Data privacy: Deep understanding of data protection regulations to ensure compliance and safeguard privacy.
- ML: Use of ML techniques to drive predictive analytics and enhance decision-making.
- Domain expertise: Insight into industry-specific data challenges and opportunities.
- Data governance: Implementation of robust data management policies to ensure data integrity and accessibility.
- Data security: Commitment to securing data assets against emerging threats.
- Data integration: Skills in synthesising disparate data sources to create a unified and powerful data ecosystem.
- Data ethics: Dedication to ethical data use, ensuring fairness and transparency.
- Data quality: Focus on maintaining the accuracy and reliability of data.
- Data strategy: Development of strategies that leverage data to drive business growth.

- Change management: Facilitating organizational shifts towards a data-centric culture.

Career pathways for advancement

Opportunities for upskilling

- Business analysts evolve into data analysts, enhancing their analytical capabilities.
- IT professionals specialise in data management and analytics, becoming key players in technological infrastructure.
- Legal experts focus on data privacy and compliance, navigating complex legal landscapes.
- Energy sector professionals transition to roles as data analysts in energy, optimising energy solutions.
- Urban planners leverage data for smart city projects, contributing to urban innovation.
- Compliance officers and compliance specialists deepen their expertise in data governance, ensuring organisational alignment with regulations.
- Data analysts enhance their skills in data integration and quality, crucial for maintaining high data standards.
- Data privacy officers champion ethical data use, setting standards for integrity and trust.
- IT managers take charge of comprehensive data management initiatives, ensuring seamless operation.
- Business strategists tailor data-driven strategies that propel businesses forward.

- HR professionals lead cultural change initiatives, embedding a data-driven mindset across organisations.

Data, often referred to as the new oil, is fuelling innovation, economic growth, and the digital transformation across industries in the GCC. Professionals in the region are uniquely positioned to harness these data-related skills, propelling their organisations into a data-driven future and unlocking new avenues for professional growth and business excellence.

IMMERSIVE TECHNOLOGIES

In the era of rapid digital transformation, one of the most captivating shifts has been the rise of immersive technologies. This term encompasses a broad range of digital solutions that create or enhance a sense of immersion, making virtual experiences feel more 'real' or augmenting the reality we perceive. As these technologies mature, they offer new avenues for business innovation, consumer engagement, and even societal change.

Understanding immersive technologies

- Virtual reality (VR): Allows users to step into a completely digital environment. Through VR headsets and sometimes additional equipment, users can experience simulated realities that can be either realistic or fantastical.

- Augmented reality (AR): Layers digital content on top of the real world, typically using smartphones or specialised glasses. This adds a layer of interactivity and information to the user's surroundings.
- Mixed reality (MR): Blends the best of VR and AR to integrate digital objects into the real world, making them interact in real time with the physical environment.

Potential applications of immersive technologies in the GCC

- Real estate and tourism: VR can offer virtual tours of properties or tourist destinations, allowing potential buyers or tourists to experience places before making a decision.
- Retail: AR can enable virtual try-ons, where consumers can see how clothes, accessories, or even makeup might look on them without physically wearing the items.
- Education: Immersive technologies can revolutionise classrooms, offering interactive 3D models, virtual field trips, and augmented textbooks.
- Healthcare: Surgeons can use MR for advanced visualisations during procedures, or therapists might use VR for immersive therapy treatments.

Challenges and considerations

- Infrastructure: Immersive technologies, especially VR, can require significant computing power and high-speed internet connections.
- User acceptance: While the younger demographic might be quick to embrace these new technologies, older generations might find them disorienting or intimidating.
- Cost implications: Developing custom VR environments or AR applications can be expensive, though prices are likely to come down as the technology becomes more widespread.
- Ethical concerns: There are potential issues related to privacy, misinformation, and even health concerns (e.g. motion sickness from VR).

Immersive technologies, while still in the early stages of global adoption, promise to redefine the ways we work, learn, and entertain ourselves. For the GCC, a region eager to position itself at the forefront of technological advancement, the potential of these technologies cannot be understated. As with all innovations, however, the journey will require vision, adaptability, and a commitment to overcoming challenges.

Skillset evolution

Professionals working with immersive technologies should have the following skills:

- VR/AR development: Proficiency in creating immersive experiences.

- 3D modelling: Ability to design 3D assets for VR/AR applications.
- User experience (UX) design: Ensuring user-friendly interactions.
- Hardware knowledge: Understanding VR/AR hardware components.
- Content creation: Developing immersive content.
- Hardware integration: Setting up VR/AR systems.
- Data analytics: Analysing user interactions.
- Cybersecurity: Ensuring data protection.
- Cost-benefit analysis: Evaluating technology investments.
- Content quality assurance: Ensuring high-quality experiences.
- Privacy compliance: Adhering to data protection laws.
- Content strategy: Planning immersive content pipelines.
- User research: Understanding user preferences.
- Legal and compliance: Navigating technology regulations.
- Innovation management: Encouraging creative solutions.

Career pathways for advancement

Existing roles for upskilling:

- Game developers: Can transition to VR/AR development.
- Graphic designers: Can specialise in 3D modelling.
- UX/UI designers: Can adapt skills for VR/AR interfaces.
- Tourism professionals: Can create virtual tourism content.
- Training instructors: Can adapt to develop VR-based training.
- IT administrators: Can specialise in VR/AR system management.

- Financial analysts: Can specialise in technology investments.
- Quality assurance testers: Can ensure immersive content quality.
- Privacy officers: Can focus on data protection.
- Cybersecurity experts: Can safeguard immersive systems.
- Content strategists: Can lead immersive content planning.
- Market researchers: Can adapt for user research.
- Legal experts: Can specialise in technology regulations.
- Innovation managers: Can drive immersive innovation.

Immersive technologies are set to revolutionise various sectors in the GCC region, offering innovative solutions for businesses and enhanced experiences for consumers. Professionals can seize opportunities by developing the skills necessary to harness the potential of these immersive technologies.

BLOCKCHAIN AND DECENTRALISED SYSTEMS

In the contemporary digital epoch, the rise of blockchain and decentralised systems has garnered substantial attention, not only for their revolutionary potential but also for the promises they hold in terms of transparency, security, and decentralised control. Here's an exploration of these groundbreaking technologies and their implications for businesses, especially in the GCC region.

Understanding blockchain and decentralised systems

Blockchain: Often described as a digital ledger, blockchain is a chain of blocks, where each block contains a number of transactions. Once a block is filled with transactions, it's linked to the previous block, forming a chain. The beauty of this technology is its transparency and immutability, ensuring that once data is stored, it cannot be tampered with.

Decentralised systems: Unlike centralised systems where a single entity has control, decentralised systems distribute control across multiple nodes or participants. This ensures greater resistance to censorship and centralised failures.

Business implications in the GCC

- Financial sector: Blockchain can revolutionise banking and finance by enabling faster, more secure transactions and cutting out middlemen, potentially saving billions. Countries like the UAE are already exploring central bank digital currencies (CBDCs).
- Supply chain: From oil and gas to luxury goods, blockchain provides traceability, ensuring authenticity and reducing counterfeit goods.
- Real estate: Blockchain could streamline property transactions, reduce fraud, and introduce more transparent property registries.

- Public services: Decentralised systems can be used for voting systems, reducing the possibility of voter fraud and enhancing democratic processes.

Challenges and considerations

- Regulatory environment: The regulatory landscape for blockchain and decentralised systems is still nascent, especially in regions like the GCC. Clear guidelines and frameworks are required to promote growth while ensuring security and legality.
- Scalability: Current leading blockchain technologies face scalability issues, limiting the number of transactions per second they can process. Solutions are being developed, but they're yet to be perfected.
- Interoperability: With multiple blockchains in existence, there's a need for these systems to interact seamlessly.

Blockchain and decentralised systems promise to redefine the fundamentals of business operations, offering transparency, security, and efficiency. The GCC, with its ambitious vision for the future, stands poised to harness this transformative power, given a strategic and informed approach.

Skillset evolution

To work effectively with blockchain and decentralised systems, professionals should possess the following skills:

- Cryptocurrency knowledge: Understanding the fundamentals of digital currencies like Bitcoin and Ethereum.
- Blockchain development: Proficiency in programming languages like Solidity for developing smart contracts.
- Cybersecurity: Strong knowledge of cryptographic techniques for securing blockchain networks.
- Distributed systems: Understanding the principles of distributed ledger technology.
- Data management: Skills in managing and analysing data stored on blockchain networks.
- Legal and compliance: Familiarity with blockchain regulations and compliance standards.

Career pathways for advancement

Existing roles for upskilling – Professionals from various roles can upskill and reskill into blockchain and decentralised systems, including:

- Software developers: Developers with experience in programming languages can transition to blockchain development.
- Cybersecurity experts: Cybersecurity professionals can extend their knowledge to blockchain security.
- Data analysts: Data analysts can learn data management on blockchain networks.
- Compliance officers: Professionals well-versed in regulations can adapt to blockchain compliance.
- Supply chain managers: Supply chain experts can explore blockchain applications in their field.

AUTOMATION AND ROBOTICS

Automation and robotics, which once graced the covers of vintage science fiction, have now become tangible instruments reshaping the fabric of industries and economies worldwide. As we venture further into this automated epoch, understanding the nuances, challenges, and opportunities of these technologies becomes paramount, especially for regions aiming to lead in innovation like the GCC.

Grasping the basics

- Automation: This refers to the use of systems, applications, or machinery to execute tasks without human intervention. Automation spans from simple tasks, like sorting emails, to complex operations, like manufacturing processes.
- Robotics: A branch of automation, robotics deals with the design, construction, and use of robots. Robots can autonomously or semi-autonomously perform tasks, guided by programming and sensory feedback.

Significance to the GCC landscape

- Manufacturing sector: The GCC, and particularly countries like the UAE and Saudi Arabia, are investing heavily in robotics to streamline manufacturing, reduce costs, and increase precision.

- Healthcare: Robot-assisted surgeries, telemedicine robots, and automated pharmacies are being explored in several GCC hospitals.
- Retail and hospitality: Automated checkout systems, robotic chefs, and service robots are entering the market, enhancing user experience and operational efficiency.
- Public infrastructure: Automation in traffic management, public transportation (like the Dubai Metro), and waste management are being implemented.

Challenges in implementation

- Economic implications: With the increase in automation, questions arise regarding job displacement. While automation does eliminate some jobs, it also creates new roles, requiring a shift in skills.
- Integration with legacy systems: Many businesses in the GCC region operate on older systems. The integration of modern robotic systems can be challenging and costly.
- Safety and security: With increased dependence on robotics, ensuring their safe operation, especially in public spaces or critical sectors like healthcare, is paramount. Additionally, these systems can be vulnerable to cyberattacks.

Recommendations for organisations

- Strategic integration: Instead of full-scale immediate adoption, a phased integration can be more effective. This would involve pilot programs, feedback loops, and iterative improvements.
- Reskilling and upskilling: To mitigate the challenge of job displacement, leaders can focus on training programs to move their workforce into roles that manage, maintain, or work alongside these automated systems.
- Collaborations: Partnering with robotics and automation startups, universities, or established tech firms can offer deep insights and accelerate adoption.
- Ethical considerations: Leaders must ensure that the adoption of automation and robotics doesn't compromise on ethical considerations, including user privacy, safety, and data protection.

Automation and robotics, while transformative, demand a nuanced approach in their integration. The GCC region, with its strategic vision and resources, has the potential to set global standards in the efficient, ethical, and innovative application of these technologies.

Skillset evolution

Professionals working with automation and robotics should have the following skills:

- Programming: Proficiency in programming languages for automation.

- Mechanical engineering: Knowledge of robot design and mechanics.
- Data analysis: Analysing data for process optimisation.
- Logistics planning: Strategising automation in supply chains.
- Healthcare operations: Integrating robotics in medical procedures.
- Safety compliance: Ensuring safe human–robot collaboration.
- Project management: Overseeing automation initiatives.
- Cost-benefit analysis: Evaluating automation investments.
- Workforce transition planning: Managing job changes incorporating human and machine responsibilities.
- Maintenance and troubleshooting: Ensuring robot functionality.
- Risk management: Mitigating operational risks.

Career pathways for advancement

Existing roles for upskilling:

- Manufacturing workers: Can transition to robot operators.
- Software developers: Can specialise in automation programming.
- Engineers: Can adapt skills for robot maintenance.
- Supply chain managers: Can adapt for logistics automation.
- Medical professionals: Can specialise in robotic surgery.
- Safety officers: Can focus on human–robot safety.
- Project managers: Can lead automation projects.
- Financial analysts: Can specialise in automation investments.
- HR professionals: Can assist in workforce transitions.

- Robot technicians: Can focus on maintenance.
- Risk managers: Can oversee operational risks.

IoT STRATEGY

IoT has emerged as a transformative force that connects everyday objects to the internet, allowing them to send, receive, and process data. This seamless interconnection promises to revolutionise the way we live, work, and even think. For regions like the GCC, which are poised at the cusp of technological advancement, understanding and integrating IoT becomes a vital stride towards a digitised future.

Decoding IoT

- Definition: IoT encompasses a network of interconnected objects embedded with sensors, software, and other technologies to connect and exchange data with other devices and systems over the internet.
- Components: The primary elements include sensors (which collect data), connectivity (to transmit this data), data processing, and user interface (to interpret and utilise the data).

IoT in the GCC landscape

- Smart cities: IoT plays a pivotal role in the development of smart cities, exemplified by initiatives like Saudi Arabia's NEOM. NEOM, envisioned as the 'land of the future', empowers the greatest minds and best talents to realise pioneering ideas and transcend boundaries in a world inspired by imagination. This ambitious project aims to optimise traffic, conserve energy, and enhance public safety through innovative IoT technologies.
- Healthcare: From wearable health monitors to smart hospital beds, IoT devices offer real-time patient monitoring, reducing risks and elevating care standards.
- Energy: The region's vast energy sector is harnessing IoT for predictive maintenance, optimised production, and efficient distribution in oil and gas facilities.
- Agriculture: Given the GCC's challenging agricultural terrain, IoT solutions like precision farming are being explored to manage water usage, monitor soil health, and predict crop yields.

Challenges and considerations

- Security concerns: With billions of interconnected devices, the potential for cyber threats multiplies, making robust security protocols a must.
- Data overload: The sheer volume of data generated can be overwhelming, necessitating efficient data processing and storage solutions.

- Interoperability: With a plethora of devices and manufacturers, ensuring seamless communication between diverse systems is crucial.
- Privacy issues: The collection of vast amounts of personal and sensitive data raises significant privacy concerns, requiring transparent data policies.

Strategic recommendations for organisations

- Invest in R&D: Understanding the rapidly evolving landscape of IoT demands R&D investments. This will foster innovation tailored to specific organisational needs.
- Partner wisely: Collaborate with trusted IoT solution providers, ensuring they align with the company's vision, values, and security standards.
- Train the workforce: As IoT devices permeate every business facet, ensuring the workforce understands their operation, benefits, and risks is essential.
- Ethical deployment: Beyond just profits and efficiency, leaders must prioritise ethical considerations, ensuring that IoT deployment respects user rights and societal wellbeing.

IoT promises a world where the boundaries between the physical and digital blur, offering unprecedented efficiency, innovation, and convenience. As the GCC marches towards a future shaped by technological prowess, integrating IoT ethically and strategically will be key to unlocking its vast potential.

Skillset evolution

Professionals developing IoT strategies should have skills in:

- IoT architecture: Designing IoT ecosystems.
- Data analytics: Extracting insights from IoT data.
- Cybersecurity: Ensuring IoT device security.
- Regulatory compliance: Navigating IoT regulations.
- Data analytics: Analysing vast amounts of IoT-generated data.
- Cybersecurity: Ensuring the security of IoT devices and networks.
- Hardware and software integration: Connecting IoT sensors and systems.
- IoT protocols: Understanding communication standards.
- Urban planning: Integrating IoT into city development.
- Agricultural science: Leveraging IoT for sustainable farming.
- IoT solution deployment: Managing IoT projects.
- Regulatory compliance: Adhering to IoT regulations.
- Privacy compliance: Navigating data privacy regulations.
- IoT standards: Ensuring compatibility and interoperability.
- Incident response: Managing IoT-related security incidents.
- Ethical IoT practices: Adhering to ethical IoT guidelines.
- Strategic planning: Defining IoT objectives and goals.
- Risk management: Assessing and mitigating IoT risks.
- Innovation management: Encouraging IoT-driven innovation.
- Change management: Facilitating IoT adoption within organisations.

Career pathways for advancement

Existing roles for reskilling:

- Architects: Can lead IoT architecture planning.
- Data analysts: Can analyse IoT-generated data.
- Cybersecurity experts: Can focus on IoT security.
- Compliance officers: Can ensure IoT regulatory compliance.
- Data analysts: Can specialise in IoT data analysis.
- IT security professionals: Can focus on IoT security.
- Engineers: Can adapt skills for IoT hardware integration.
- Network administrators: Can manage IoT network protocols.
- Urban planners: Can lead IoT integration in city planning.
- Agricultural experts: Can specialise in IoT-based agriculture.
- Project managers: Can oversee IoT deployment.
- Compliance officers: Can ensure IoT regulatory adherence.
- Legal experts: Can specialise in IoT privacy compliance.
- IoT standards specialists: Can ensure interoperability.
- Incident response teams: Can manage IoT security incidents.
- Ethics officers: Can enforce ethical IoT practices.
- Strategists: Can lead IoT strategy development.
- Risk analysts: Can assess IoT-related risks.
- Innovation managers: Can promote IoT-driven innovation.
- Change agents and managers: Can facilitate IoT adoption.

IoT is reshaping industries in the GCC region, offering unprecedented opportunities for optimisation and innovation. Professionals can prepare for this technological revolution by acquiring the necessary skills to harness IoT's potential and overcome associated challenges.

CYBERSECURITY

In an era where data is the most valuable commodity and our world is more interconnected than ever, cybersecurity has risen as an indispensable pillar of digital transformation. As the backbone of safe digital operations, cybersecurity ensures that businesses, governments, and individuals are protected against malicious threats. For regions like the GCC, with a burgeoning digital landscape, fortifying cybersecurity measures becomes not just a need but a critical mandate.

Understanding cybersecurity

- Definition: Cybersecurity refers to the practice of protecting computer systems, networks, programs, and data from digital attacks, unauthorised access, damage, or theft.
- Key concepts: This encompasses information security (protecting data's integrity), network security (defending a computer network), application security (ensuring apps are secure), and operational security (processes to protect data during operations).

Cybersecurity in the GCC landscape

- National strategy: Countries like UAE and Saudi Arabia have launched national cybersecurity strategies, emphasising the sector's importance in national development.
- Infrastructure: Given the GCC's critical infrastructure in energy and finance, robust cybersecurity is essential to protect against potentially catastrophic attacks.
- Digital commerce: As e-commerce grows, ensuring safe transactions and customer data protection is vital.
- Public services: With a push towards e-governance, ensuring citizens' data is protected against breaches is paramount.

Challenges and risks

- Rapid digital growth: The swift pace of digital transformation in the GCC can sometimes outpace the speed of implementing adequate cybersecurity measures.
- Sophisticated attacks: Modern cyberattacks, including state-sponsored attacks, are growing in complexity and sophistication.
- Skills gap: The cybersecurity field often faces a shortage of adequately trained professionals to tackle emerging threats.
- Compliance and regulation: Keeping up with international and regional cybersecurity standards can be challenging.

Actionable insights for organisations

- Continuous education: Cybersecurity is not a one-time solution but a continual process. Leaders must invest in ongoing education and training for their teams.
- Incident response planning: Have a proactive approach with a well-drafted incident response plan to manage potential breaches.
- Collaborative defence: Partner with cybersecurity firms, government bodies, and international entities for shared intelligence and best practices.
- Prioritise investment: Cybersecurity is not an area to cut corners. Adequate budget allocation ensures that the best tools, practices, and professionals safeguard the organisation.
- Promote a culture of security: From the entry-level employee to top management, everyone should be ingrained with a mindset of security first.

Cybersecurity, in the modern digital realm, is akin to the walls and moats of ancient fortresses. As the GCC propels into a digital future, the sanctity of its digital realms will hinge on robust, adaptive, and vigilant cybersecurity practices. Leaders, as guardians of their organisations, carry the mantle of ensuring this sanctity, making cybersecurity an unyielding priority.

Skillset evolution

Professionals working in cybersecurity should possess a diverse skillset that includes:

- Network security: Securing network infrastructure.
- Threat analysis: Identifying and assessing cyber threats.
- Incident response: Responding to and mitigating security incidents.
- Compliance and regulation: Ensuring adherence to cybersecurity laws and regulations.
- Critical infrastructure protection: Safeguarding vital systems.
- Security risk assessment: Evaluating cyber risks.
- Security policy development: Creating and implementing security policies.
- International cybersecurity cooperation: Collaborating on global security issues.
- Threat intelligence: Staying informed about emerging threats.
- Security awareness training: Educating employees about cybersecurity.
- Innovation in security: Adopting new security technologies.
- Legal and ethical cybersecurity practices: Ensuring compliance and ethics.
- Strategic cybersecurity planning: Developing comprehensive security strategies.
- Technology evaluation: Assessing and implementing cybersecurity technologies.
- Employee training: Providing ongoing cybersecurity education.
- Crisis management: Responding effectively to security incidents.

Career pathways for advancement

Existing roles for upskilling:

- IT professionals: Can specialise in network security.
- Analysts: Can transition into threat analysis roles.
- IT support teams: Can expand into incident response teams.
- Legal and compliance experts: Can focus on cybersecurity compliance.
- System administrators: Can specialise in critical infrastructure protection.
- Risk assessors: Can assess and manage cybersecurity risks.
- Policy analysts: Can contribute to security policy development.
- Diplomats: Can engage in international cybersecurity diplomacy.
- Threat analysts: Can specialise in threat intelligence.
- Training specialists: Can conduct security awareness training.
- Innovators: Can explore and implement new security solutions.
- Legal and ethical experts: Can ensure cybersecurity practices are legal and ethical.
- Cybersecurity strategists: Can lead security planning efforts.
- Technology evaluators: Can assess and implement cybersecurity tools.
- Cybersecurity trainers: Can educate employees about security.
- Crisis managers: Can lead incident response teams.

Cybersecurity is a paramount concern for organisations and governments in the GCC region as they navigate the complexities of the digital age. Professionals with expertise in cybersecurity are instrumental in protecting critical infrastructure and ensuring the secure operation of digital systems.

As we conclude our in-depth exploration of the transformative technologies in Chapter 7, it becomes clear that understanding these innovations is only one piece of the puzzle. The next step in our journey is presented in Chapter 8, where we dive into global best practices, stepping outside the confines of technology-specific discussions to examine how different regions and industries across the globe have successfully implemented digital strategies and fostered digital competencies.

GLOBAL BEST PRACTICES

I n the quest to bridge the digital skills gap, organisations can gain immensely from examining global best practices. By looking beyond regional confines, one can identify patterns of success and strategies that have effectively nurtured digital prowess in diverse workforces. This section delves into some noteworthy initiatives and models from around the world that have set benchmarks in digital skills development.

GLOBAL BEST PRACTICE: AI INITIATIVES IN CHINA

China's rapid ascent in the global AI arena is a testimony to its strategic focus, vast data resources, and commitment to innovation. Through a harmonious blend of government support, entrepreneurial spirit, and infrastructure development, China aims to establish itself as the world leader in AI by 2030. This case study dissects the elements underpinning China's AI surge, offering valuable insights for GCC leaders.

Origins of China's AI boom

- Government strategy: The 'New Generation Artificial Intelligence Development Plan' is China's roadmap for AI dominance and details its objectives of fostering AI innovation, integrating AI into industries and public services, and creating a global AI cooperation framework.

- Data advantage: This strategy examines China's massive digital user base and how its data-rich environment acts as a fertile ground for AI development and implementation.
- Startup ecosystem: This ecosystem highlights the role of thriving tech hubs like Beijing and Shenzhen, which have become breeding grounds for AI startups.

Noteworthy AI projects and implementations

- SenseTime's AI-driven solutions: This project shows the advancements made by this tech giant, renowned for its facial recognition technology, which plays a pivotal role in public security, financial services, and retail in China.
- Alibaba's City Brain: This cloud computing and AI-powered platform was designed to enhance urban governance by optimising city services such as traffic management.
- Baidu's Apollo: This open-source autonomous driving platform represents China's ambition to be at the forefront of the self-driving vehicle revolution.

Collaborative ecosystem

- AI research institutes: Institutions such as the Tencent AI Lab and Alibaba's DAMO Academy, which are pioneering cutting-edge AI research and facilitating collaborations between academia and industry.

- Public–private partnerships: An exploration of the symbiotic relationships formed between tech giants like Huawei and government entities to promote AI-driven societal and economic advancements.

Learning for the GCC

- Learning from scale: Provides insights into how China's large-scale AI implementations can be adapted for GCC nations, considering regional contexts and specificities.
- Public policy and regulation: Understanding the fine balance China maintains between AI advancement and ethical considerations.
- Investment and collaboration opportunities: Identifying avenues for GCC businesses and governments to collaborate with Chinese AI entities, facilitating knowledge transfer and technological adoption.

China's AI narrative offers a wealth of knowledge for GCC leaders eager to harness AI's potential. By studying China's strategic approach, embracing its emphasis on collaboration, and recognising the power of a supportive policy environment, the GCC can envision and actualise its AI-driven future, harmoniously aligned with nationalisation goals.

GLOBAL BEST PRACTICE: BLOCKCHAIN ADOPTION IN ESTONIA

Estonia, a small Baltic nation, stands tall as a testament to the transformative power of technology. With its pioneering e-residency program and a national drive to digitise public services, Estonia has integrated blockchain technology in various sectors, ensuring data integrity, transparency, and efficiency. This case study unravels Estonia's journey with blockchain, serving as an exemplar for GCC leaders.

Genesis of Estonia's digital ambition

- Early adopters: Estonia, after its independence from the Soviet Union in 1991, embraced digital solutions to leapfrog its development and integrate itself into the global economy.
- e-Estonia initiative: Introduced a national program aimed at digitising all public services, from voting to health records, culminating in the e-residency program that grants digital identity to global citizens.

Blockchain's role in e-Estonia

- KSI blockchain: Estonia's deployment of keyless signature infrastructure (KSI) blockchain ensures the security, integrity, and continuity of digital records and systems across the public sector.

- Data embassies: Through an innovative concept, Estonia stores critical data backups in 'data embassies' located in partner countries, safeguarded by blockchain to ensure data immutability.

Flagship blockchain implementations

- Digital identity: The e-residency program, a blockchain-backed digital identity available to anyone globally, allows users to start and manage businesses in Estonia.
- Health records: Estonia's digital health record system leverages blockchain to grant patients control over their data, ensuring its accuracy and security while enabling seamless sharing among healthcare providers.
- Land registry and real estate: Integration of blockchain in managing land titles and property transactions, ensuring transparency and safeguarding against fraud.

Key takeaways for the GCC

- Scalability: Estonia's ability to implement large-scale digital solutions despite its small size, emphasising the scalability and adaptability of blockchain technology.

- Public trust and engagement: Understanding the importance of cultivating public trust in digital systems, an area where Estonia excels, offering lessons for GCC nations embarking on similar digital journeys.
- Partnerships and collaborative frameworks: Recognising the value of multi-stakeholder collaborations, from tech providers to academic institutions, that have been instrumental in Estonia's blockchain success.

Estonia's blockchain story underscores the potency of a strategic, nation-wide approach to technological adoption. For GCC leaders, Estonia's successes and challenges offer a roadmap, illustrating how blockchain can be intricately woven into the national fabric, simultaneously advancing digital transformation objectives.

GLOBAL BEST PRACTICE: ECOSYSTEM COLLABORATION

One of the pivotal aspects of bridging the digital skills gap while achieving nationalisation goals is the integration of the entire ecosystem. This comprises governments, businesses, educational institutions, and the wider community. When all these entities collaborate harmoniously, they create a robust framework to nurture digital literacy and competencies, beginning from a young age and persisting throughout one's career.

Why ecosystem collaboration matters

Ecosystem collaboration is not just a trend, but a necessity. When different facets of society collaborate, the following is possible:

- Unified vision: Creates a shared understanding of national and digital objectives.
- Efficient resource utilisation: Avoids duplication of efforts and ensures that resources are utilised in areas with the highest impact.
- Adaptive learning: Ensures that the skills taught in educational institutions are relevant to the demands of the business world.

The Nordic model

The Nordic countries, comprising Denmark, Finland, Iceland, Norway, and Sweden, offer a compelling case study in ecosystem collaboration.

- Holistic approach: The Nordics prioritise digital literacy from the earliest stages of education. The curriculum is consistently updated to include new technologies and methodologies.
- Public–private partnerships: Governments and businesses come together to sponsor research, innovations, and training programs.

- Lifelong learning: Adult education programs ensure that even older generations are not left behind in the digital revolution. This is made possible through community centres, online platforms, and workplace initiatives.

The German dual training system

Germany's vocational training system offers another model of successful ecosystem collaboration.

- Theory meets practice: Students split their time between classroom instruction at a vocational school and practical training at a company.
- Industry-relevant curriculum: Since businesses are directly involved in training, the skills imparted are immediately relevant to real-world demands.
- Employment assurance: Students often secure positions within their training company post-graduation, ensuring a seamless transition from education to employment.

The role of tech giants

Several multinational technology corporations recognise the need for ecosystem collaboration and have taken significant steps in this direction.

- Collaborative platforms: Tools like Microsoft Teams or Google Workspace not only facilitate digital operations but also actively collaborate with educational institutions to offer training.
- Funding and grants: Companies provide funding for tech initiatives, research, and digital skills training in educational institutions.
- Public policy influence: By working closely with governments, these corporations help in shaping digital education policies, ensuring they are up to date and relevant.

Ecosystem collaboration stands as a testament to the adage, 'The whole is greater than the sum of its parts'. When each entity of the ecosystem – be it the government, educational institution, business, or community – collaborates towards a unified goal of digital empowerment, the results can be transformative. Organisations in the GCC can draw inspiration from these models, adapting them to their unique contexts to create an inclusive and tech-empowered society.

ECOSYSTEM COLLABORATION: PRIVATE SECTOR INITIATIVES

In the intricate tapestry of the digital transformation narrative, private sector companies stand as influential weavers, intricately shaping the direction, depth, and pace of change. These entities not only adapt to the digital revolution but are often at the vanguard, pushing boundaries and setting the pace. Their initiatives are crucial in addressing the digital skills gap, given their unique position of understanding market needs, technological advancements, and workforce dynamics.

The imperative of private sector engagement

Private sector initiatives in digital skills development are not just about corporate social responsibility or brand building; they are fundamentally about business survival, competitiveness, and future growth.

- Market-driven adaptability: The private sector, being market-driven, is acutely aware of the evolving digital skill needs.
- Talent pool development: By investing in digital skills training, companies ensure a steady stream of qualified employees for their future needs.
- Innovation and competitive edge: Companies that foster a digitally competent workforce are more likely to innovate and maintain a competitive edge in the market.

Tech giants taking charge

Prominent technology companies have spearheaded significant initiatives to promote digital literacy and competency.

- Google's Grow with Google: An initiative aimed at providing free training, tools, and resources to help individuals grow their skills, career, or business.
- Microsoft's Global Skills Initiative: Aimed at bringing more digital skills to 25 million people worldwide by offering free access to learning content.
- Amazon's Upskilling 2025: A pledge to invest US$700 million to upskill 100,000 of its employees in the United States, guiding them towards in-demand jobs and highly skilled roles.

Partnerships and collaborations

Many private sector companies have realised that partnerships amplify impact. These collaborations often span across sectors and borders.

- IBM's P-TECH model: In partnership with governments and educational institutions, this initiative offers students an integrated high school and college curriculum, focusing on STEM skills, and ensures they're industry-ready.
- Cisco Networking Academy: Partners with educational institutions globally to provide digital skills and IT training courses.

In-house training and reskilling

Beyond external initiatives, private-sector companies are heavily investing in their in-house training programs.

- Accenture's New Skills Now: A strategy focused on training its workforce in the newest digital technologies, including blockchain, AI, and advanced analytics.
- Deloitte University: A state-of-the-art learning facility where employees are trained in various disciplines, including digital transformations.

Private sector initiatives are instrumental in bridging the digital skills gap. For the GCC region, these endeavours can act as catalysts, accelerating the process of nationalisation by ensuring that local talent is not just employed, but also competent, innovative, and ready to lead in the digital era. As the private sector continues to play a leading role in this domain, it reinforces the belief that the future workforce's competency is a shared responsibility, one that transcends corporate boundaries and enters the realm of collective societal progress.

As we move on from the global perspectives and case studies of Chapter 8, we've gleaned valuable insights on the successful strategies and initiatives that have propelled nations and organisations to the forefront of digital transformation. Next, in Chapter 9, we turn our attention to applying these global best practices within the unique context of the GCC nations.

CHAPTER 9

BUILDING DIGITAL COMPETENCIES ROADMAP

The nations of the GCC find themselves confronting the task of nurturing and developing an infrastructure abundant in digital competencies amid this evolving landscape.

To fully understand this transformation, it's essential to differentiate between digital skills and digital competencies. Digital skills refer to the practical abilities enabling individuals to use digital tools effectively. These are typically task-specific skills such as coding, data analysis, or the ability to use particular software.

Contrarily, digital competencies incorporate a more extensive set of capabilities, transcending mere skills. These include attitudes, knowledge, strategies, and critical understanding necessary to exploit digital technologies in a comprehensive and context-specific manner. This extends to the adaptability to use new digital tools, understanding the repercussions of digital technologies, and the ability to use these technologies safely and responsibly.

For the GCC nations, the broader concept of digital competencies is what needs to be nurtured in order to fortify this digital ecosystem. An effective economy and a prosperous society in the digital age demand more than just individual skills; they necessitate a comprehensive understanding and utilisation of digital technologies, deeply intertwined with the cultural, social, and economic aspects of the region. This chapter provides organisations with a detailed roadmap to develop a holistic approach to digital competency development and skill development, embedding digital literacy and expertise into the very fabric of their organisations.

COMPETENCY-BUILDING ROADMAP

1. Identifying organisational needs

- Environmental scan: Continuously monitor industry trends, consumer preferences, competitor actions, and technological advancements. This helps identify necessary industry-specific competencies and fosters a culture of growth.
- Technology roadmap: Create a clear technology roadmap by assessing current capabilities and projecting future tech demands, aligning it with organisational competencies for seamless integration.
- Stakeholder collaboration: Engage department heads and team leaders to understand specific digital needs within each domain, ensuring a tailored approach to competency development.

- Skills audit: Use tools and surveys to assess your workforce's current digital proficiency, in conjunction with soft and technical skills already within the organisation.
- Gap analysis: Compare current skills with industry benchmarks and organisational goals to pinpoint areas needing improvement.
- Competency framework: Analyse current skills and competencies against future needs. Identify skill gaps and use this analysis to develop training programs and hiring strategies for adaptability and innovation.

2. Creating a digital learning ecosystem

- Digital learning platforms: Invest in or collaborate with platforms in learning experience platforms such as Disprz as well as other industry-specific platforms for curated digital courses accessible to all employees.
- Internal knowledge sharing: Promote regular workshops and webinars where in-house experts or external subject-matter experts share insights and skills on industry-specific digital advancements.
- Digital learning libraries: Build a repository of resources, guides, and courses that are industry- or organisation-specific and accessible to all employees.
- Partnership programs: Form alliances with universities and technical institutions to develop courses tailored to your industry's needs.
- Internships and apprenticeships: Establish robust programs that allow employees and students to gain practical experience while infusing fresh digital perspectives into your

organisation. This can be a two-way exchange by allowing students studying key tech or digital disciplines to work in your organisation and create a pipeline of talent. Similarly, employees reskilling into tech disciplines could apprentice externally in startups or internally in digital transformations to apply their skills in real-time projects in the business.

- Guest lectures and workshops: Invite academics, scholars, and industry experts to conduct sessions, fostering a bridge between academia and industry.

3. Employee engagement and feedback

- Feedback mechanisms: Create platforms for employees to share feedback on training programs, ensuring these programs are aligned with their needs.
- Engagement metrics: Monitor indicators like course completion rates, internal or external placement of reskilled staff, application of learnt skills, and overall employee satisfaction and attrition.
- Iterative improvement: Use feedback to continually refine training methodologies and content.

4. Fostering a digital mindset

- Top-down leadership: Ensure that digital enthusiasm is evident at the leadership level, setting a precedent for the entire organisation.
- Reward and recognition: Implement systems to acknowledge and incentivise employees who demonstrate exemplary digital skills or continuous learning.

- Collaborative culture: Promote a culture where employees are encouraged to share digital insights, collaborate on tech projects, and support each other's digital journeys.

Building digital competencies is a continuous journey, not a destination. It is supported by adopting a continuous learning culture to ensure organisations remain agile, adaptable, and future-ready, aligning seamlessly with nationalisation goals and carving a niche in the digital realm of the GCC.

EMPLOYEE DEVELOPMENT FOR CULTIVATING A FUTURE-READY WORKFORCE

In a digital age, preparing employees for future challenges is not limited to traditional training. It involves holistic strategies that combine academic insights with real-world applications. This chapter underscores strategies that GCC leaders can employ to ensure a workforce that's agile, innovative, and ready for the challenges and opportunities of the digital era.

1. Harnessing the power of apprenticeships and internships

- Real-world skill application: Apprenticeships and internships provide an unparalleled platform for hands-on, application-based training. They allow employees to test and apply what they've learnt in a real-world setting, bridging the gap between theoretical knowledge and practical application.

- Accelerated skill acquisition: Such programs can drastically shorten the time required to close the digital skills gap. By providing immediate feedback and iterative learning experiences, they offer a fast-tracked, immersive learning curve.

2. Collaboration with startups for on-ground digital experience

- Tapping into innovation: Startups often operate at the cutting edge of technology and innovation. Collaborating with them provides employees with exposure to the latest in digital trends, tools, and methodologies.
- Mutually beneficial partnerships: While employees gain valuable insights, startups benefit from the expertise, resources, and structured processes that established organisations bring. It's a synergy where innovation meets experience.

3. Strategic partnerships with educational bodies

- Tailored industry education: Collaborating with universities and educational institutions ensures the curriculum is tailored to address specific industry needs. Such partnerships result in programs that are more aligned with the actual demands of the business world.
- Continuous curriculum evolution: The digital landscape is ever-evolving. These partnerships allow for a continuous feedback loop, ensuring that educational content remains updated and relevant.

4. Recognising and nurturing in-house talent

- Skill audits: Periodically assess the existing skills within the organisation to identify strengths and areas that need enhancement.
- Personalised development plans: With insights from these audits, formulate tailored development plans that cater to both the organisation's future goals and the individual's professional aspirations.

5. Modern learning and real-world application

- Blended learning paradigms: A mix of traditional classroom sessions, digital courses, and experiential learning ensures a well-rounded development.
- Project rotations: Encourage employees to rotate between different projects, allowing them to apply diverse skills and gain a holistic understanding of the business.

6. Fostering a resilient and adaptable workforce

- Soft skills enhancement: Beyond technical acumen, focus on developing soft skills like critical thinking, adaptability, and emotional intelligence.
- Feedback mechanisms: Constructive feedback after task completion or project milestones helps employees refine their approach and grow.

7. Celebrating achievements and embracing failures

- Recognition and rewards: Acknowledge employees who show growth, innovation, and proactivity.
- Learning from mistakes: Cultivate an environment where setbacks are viewed as learning opportunities, fostering a culture of continuous improvement.

In essence, creating a future-ready workforce in the GCC region requires a multi-pronged approach that extends beyond traditional training. It involves embracing new methodologies, seeking external collaborations, and most importantly, ensuring that learning and development are iterative, practical, and aligned with the real-world digital landscape.

GLOBAL BEST PRACTICE: IBM'S P-TECH

In the dynamic world of business and technology, some organisations stand out as pioneers in employee development and skilling. IBM's P-TECH (Pathways in Technology Early College High School) is one such groundbreaking initiative that redefines the integration of education and industry, paving the way for a future-ready workforce (IBM, 2020).

Overview of P-TECH

- Foundational idea: P-TECH is a collaborative educational model that bridges the gap between high school, college, and professional worlds, offering students an integrated six-year program to earn a high school diploma, an industry-recognised associate degree, and relevant work experience in STEM fields.
- Key players: P-TECH represents a unique partnership between public high schools, community colleges, and leading businesses like IBM.
- Global presence: Since its inception in New York, in 2011, the model has expanded to various countries, signifying its adaptability and success across diverse cultures and education systems.

Features and benefits

- Workplace learning: Students get exposure to the corporate world through internships, mentorships, and job shadowing, giving them practical insights early in their careers.
- Industry-relevant curriculum: Courses are co-developed by educators and industry professionals, ensuring that the skills imparted are pertinent to current industry needs.
- Cost-effective model: By combining high school and college curriculums, P-TECH offers students a pathway to a degree and career without the

financial burdens commonly associated with tertiary education.

Impact on digital skills development

- Tailored training: Given IBM's significant role in the tech industry, students are provided with training that's finely attuned to the demands of the digital era. This includes areas like cloud computing, AI, and cybersecurity.
- Mentorship from experts: P-TECH students are paired with IBM professionals, receiving first-hand insights into the nuances of tech roles and responsibilities.
- Career kickstart: Graduates are first in line for job considerations at IBM, effectively bridging the skills gap from both the educational and the employment perspectives.

Relevance to the GCC context

- Potential for collaboration: With its emphasis on public–private partnerships, the P-TECH model could serve as a blueprint for collaborations between GCC governments, educational institutions, and businesses.
- Filling the skills gap: By introducing such integrated educational models in the GCC, there's potential to nurture a workforce that's not just academically sound

but also industry-ready, addressing the region's unique nationalisation and digital competency challenges.

- Regional adaptability: The success of P-TECH in various countries suggests that it can be adapted to the specific educational and industrial needs of the GCC.

IBM's P-TECH serves as a testament to the power of collaboration in moulding a future-ready workforce. It's a beacon for leaders and policymakers in the GCC, illustrating that with foresight, innovation, and partnership, it's possible to reconcile nationalisation goals with the imperatives of the digital age, creating a talent pipeline from high school.

FRAMEWORK: 3C FRAMEWORK

In the rapidly evolving landscape of digital transformation, building robust digital competencies requires a structured and comprehensive approach. The 3C Framework has been designed as a practical tool for leaders to address this challenge, encompassing three crucial pillars: culture, capability, and collaboration. Here's a detailed exploration of this framework:

Culture

Definition: Establishing a company-wide culture that values continuous learning, innovation, and adaptability.

This cultural alignment acts as the bedrock for any digital transformation effort.

Key strategies

- Leadership commitment: Senior management should exemplify a digital-first mindset and champion the need for digital competence and curiosity.
- Reward and recognition: Introduce incentives for employees who upskill, innovate, or contribute significantly to digital initiatives.
- Open communication: Encourage a feedback-driven environment where employees can share their challenges and suggestions regarding digital adoption.

Benefits

- Enhanced employee engagement in digital initiatives.
- Faster adoption of digital tools and practices.
- Reduction in resistance to change.

Capability

Definition: Focusing on developing the right skills and knowledge needed to harness the power of digital technologies effectively.

Key strategies

- Training programs: Offer courses tailored to specific roles, ensuring relevance and applicability.

- Knowledge sharing: Host regular seminars, webinars, or workshops where internal or external experts share insights on emerging technologies.
- Digital toolkits: Provide employees with access to tools, resources, and platforms that aid in their digital learning journey.

Benefits

- A workforce that's equipped to handle current and future digital challenges.
- Streamlined operations and improved efficiencies due to enhanced digital capabilities.
- Retention of top talent who value personal and professional growth.

Collaboration

Definition: Encouraging cross-departmental, interdisciplinary, and even cross-industry collaborations to derive maximum value from digital initiatives.

Key strategies

- Collaborative platforms: Implement tools like Microsoft Teams or Slack to facilitate seamless communication and collaboration.
- Cross-functional teams: Create teams comprising members from diverse departments to work on specific digital projects, ensuring varied perspectives.

- Industry partnerships: Collaborate with external tech firms, startups, or academia to drive innovation and gain fresh insights.

Benefits

- Harnessing the collective intelligence of the organisation.
- Breaking down silos, leading to a more integrated and cohesive digital strategy.
- Access to external expertise and innovative solutions through partnerships.

The 3C Framework provides a holistic approach for leaders to build a digitally competent organisation. By focusing on culture, capability, and collaboration, companies can ensure that they're not only equipped to tackle the challenges of the digital era but also poised to seize the myriad opportunities it presents.

As we turn the page to Chapter 10, we embark on a journey to understand and embrace the future of work – a future where human potential, augmented by machine capabilities, opens new horizons of possibilities and achievements.

HUMAN–MACHINE COLLABORATION

In an age where machines are becoming increasingly sophisticated, the boundaries between human tasks and machine tasks are blurring. This chapter delves into the symbiotic relationship between humans and machines, exploring how organisations can optimise their workforce by fostering effective human–machine collaboration.

INTRODUCTION: THE PARADIGM SHIFT

The digital age has ushered in a series of profound changes that are redefining the ways we perceive work, productivity, and collaboration. Among the most transformative of these is the evolving dynamic between humans and machines. Historically, machinery was invented to assist humans, to simplify manual tasks, and to increase productivity. As time progressed, and with the advent of the computer age, machines transformed from mere tools of assistance to being perceived as potential rivals, threatening job security across various sectors. Today, we stand on the cusp of yet another shift: the age of human–machine collaboration.

This paradigm shift is not one of humans versus machines but rather humans *with* machines. The future isn't about creating independent AI entities but is centred around AI augmenting human capabilities. Imagine a pianist and a violinist. Independently, each can produce beautiful music, but together, they can create a symphony. Similarly, humans and machines, with their distinct capabilities, can produce outcomes that neither could achieve alone.

At the core of this change is the recognition that machines, no matter how sophisticated, lack the emotional intelligence, nuanced understanding, creativity, and strategic foresight inherent to humans. On the other hand, humans can't match the sheer data-processing power, precision, and computational prowess of machines.

Redefining roles in the face of this collaboration is paramount. No longer is the narrative about machines replacing human jobs. Instead, it's about machines enhancing human capabilities, freeing us from mundane and repetitive tasks, and allowing us to focus on what we do best: think, create, strategise, and innovate. This new form of collaboration can lead to increased productivity, greater innovation, and a more meaningful work experience for humans.

The transition, however, requires a reimagining of traditional organisational structures and roles. It calls for a clear understanding of the strengths and limitations of both parties and a roadmap for their effective integration.

As we delve deeper into this chapter, we will explore the nuances of this collaboration, providing insights into how organisations can harness the combined strength of humans and machines to create a future-ready, optimised workforce. This journey begins with understanding and appreciating the unique strengths of both entities and learning how, in unison, they can redefine the boundaries of what's possible.

UNDERSTANDING HUMAN AND MACHINE STRENGTHS

In order to orchestrate a harmonious collaboration between humans and machines, it's imperative to comprehend the unique strengths each brings to the table. This knowledge serves as the foundation for determining which tasks are best suited for humans, which for machines, and where the collaboration can produce synergy.

FIGURE 5. ACCENTURE

Human strengths

1. Emotional intelligence: Humans are uniquely equipped to understand and navigate the complex web of emotions, motivations, and interpersonal dynamics. This allows us to build relationships, navigate social situations, and make decisions based on nuanced emotional considerations.

2. Creativity: The human mind is inherently imaginative. We can dream, innovate, and envision possibilities beyond current realities. Machines can process and analyse, but they cannot truly create in the way humans can.

3. Strategic foresight: While machines can predict based on patterns and data, humans excel at strategic thinking. We have the ability to anticipate long-term consequences, make decisions in the face of uncertainty, and navigate situations that lack precedent.

4. Ethical judgement: Morality, values, and ethics are innately human constructs. When faced with decisions that require a moral or ethical standpoint, human judgement is indispensable.

5. Adaptability: Humans can adjust to new information, unexpected challenges, and changing environments with a versatility that machines currently cannot emulate.

Machine strengths

1. Data processing: Machines, especially with the rise of advanced AI, can process vast amounts of data at speeds incomprehensible to humans. This allows for efficient analysis, pattern recognition, and prediction.

2. Precision and consistency: Once programmed, machines can perform tasks with an unparalleled level of precision and consistency, eliminating human errors due to fatigue or oversight.

3. Endurance: Machines don't experience fatigue, emotion, or distraction. They can work continuously without

breaks, making them ideal for tasks that require sustained attention.

4. Multitasking: Computers can simultaneously manage multiple tasks efficiently, something the human brain struggles with.

5. Complex calculations: For tasks that require intricate mathematical calculations or simulations, machines are unmatched in their speed and accuracy.

THE SYNERGY OF COLLABORATION

When we view these strengths side by side, it becomes evident that humans and machines complement each other. For instance, in a healthcare setting, a machine can quickly analyse a patient's symptoms and medical history, in conjunction with the latest medical research, to suggest a diagnosis. However, it's the doctor's role to communicate this diagnosis, consider the emotional and psychological implications for the patient, and make ethical decisions regarding treatment.

In business, while machines can analyse market trends and provide data-driven insights, human leaders must use these insights to strategise, innovate, and make complex decisions considering a multitude of non-quantifiable factors.

The future lies not in choosing between human and machine, but in leveraging the strengths of both. By understanding and respecting what each brings to the table, organisations can reimagine roles and processes to create a collaborative framework that maximises efficiency, innovation, and value.

Designing the collaborative workforce

The nexus of human and machine collaboration requires thoughtful orchestration to create a workforce that is adaptive, synergistic, and geared towards optimal productivity. Designing such a workforce is not just about integrating technology into operations; it's about cultivating an environment where both human talents and machine capabilities are utilised to their fullest potential. Here's how organisations can pave the way for this integrated future:

1. Role reimagining

Task allocation: Begin by dissecting job roles into tasks and categorising them based on their nature. Which tasks require human empathy, creativity, or complex decision-making? Which ones rely on data processing, precision, or repetitiveness? By understanding the essence of each task, it becomes clearer where machine intervention would be most beneficial.

Job enrichment: With automation taking over certain tasks, humans are free to engage in more complex, value-added activities. This means job roles can evolve to be more strategic, innovative, and impactful, leading to increased job satisfaction and meaningful contributions.

2. Skill development and continuous learning

Embrace lifelong learning: As machines evolve, so should the human workforce. Encourage continuous learning where employees are regularly updating their skills, particularly in areas like digital literacy, data interpretation, and human–machine interaction.

Training initiatives: Invest in training programs that don't just focus on how to use technology, but on how to collaborate with it. Such programs should instil an understanding of machine logic, the principles behind AI and automation, and their implications in the workplace.

3. Technology as a partner

User-friendly interfaces: For effective collaboration, the interfaces and platforms through which humans interact with machines should be intuitive and user-friendly. This ensures a smooth interaction and reduces the learning curve.

Feedback loops: Implement systems where machines provide feedback based on data and patterns, and humans provide feedback based on their experiences and observations. This two-way feedback mechanism ensures continuous improvement.

4. Fostering a collaborative culture

Inclusivity: A culture that values both human and machine contributions equally is pivotal. This means celebrating the insights a machine provides just as much as human innovations and ensuring that credit is shared.

Interdisciplinary teams: Form teams that blend tech experts with professionals from other disciplines. This not only promotes mutual respect and understanding but also leads to richer insights and more comprehensive problem-solving.

5. Ethical considerations and governance

Transparent policies: As machines take on more roles, it's crucial to have clear policies on data usage, ML ethics, and decision-making authority. Who is accountable if a machine makes an error? How is data being used and protected?

Ethical training: Ensure that the human workforce understands the ethical implications of working alongside machines, especially when it comes to data privacy, security, and potential biases in ML models.

6. Infrastructure and tools

Invest in robust technologies: While the allure of cutting-edge technologies is undeniable, it's essential to invest in tools and platforms that align with your organisation's needs and can scale with growth.

Hybrid workspaces: Design work environments that cater to both human comfort and machine efficiency. This includes everything from physical collaboration spaces for the human workforce to optimal server rooms for computational needs.

7. Measure, evaluate, and iterate

Performance metrics: Traditional performance indicators may not suffice in this new collaborative paradigm. Develop metrics that measure the efficiency and productivity of human–machine collaborations, ensuring that they account for quality, innovation, and adaptability.

Regular evaluations: Periodically review the state of collaboration in your organisation. Are there areas where the balance is off? Are there emerging technologies that could be integrated?

In conclusion, designing the collaborative workforce is an intricate dance of blending the analytical prowess of machines with the intuitive genius of humans. When orchestrated effectively, this integration promises unparalleled efficiency, creativity, and growth, heralding a future where the sum of human–machine collaboration is undeniably greater than its individual parts.

ETHICAL CONSIDERATIONS IN COLLABORATION

In the embrace of the human–machine collaborative future, ethical considerations rise prominently on the horizon. While technology has the potential to enhance operations, decision-making, and even user experiences, it also brings to the fore a myriad of ethical challenges that organisations must navigate judiciously. This section delves deep into the key ethical facets of this collaboration, offering insights on how to approach them conscientiously.

1. Data privacy and protection

Respecting user data: As machines process vast quantities of data, ensuring the privacy and security of this data becomes paramount. It's essential to establish clear guidelines regarding data collection, storage, sharing, and utilisation, ensuring that user data is always handled with respect and integrity.

Consent and transparency: Users must be informed about how their data will be used and must provide explicit consent. This extends beyond mere legal compliance to fostering trust with users, partners, and stakeholders.

2. Accountability and responsibility

Decision-making oversight: Machines, especially AI-driven ones, will make decisions based on the data and algorithms they're fed. However, when an unexpected decision or error occurs, who is held accountable? Clear lines of accountability must be established to handle such eventualities.

Continuous monitoring: Systems should be in place to continuously monitor and review machine decisions, ensuring they align with organisational values and ethical considerations.

3. Bias and fairness

Algorithmic bias: ML models are trained on data, and if this data contains biases (often reflective of historical or societal biases), the machine will perpetuate these biases. Efforts must be made to recognise, understand, and rectify biased data and algorithms.

Diverse datasets: To counteract potential biases, datasets used for training should be diverse, representative, and continually reviewed for fairness and accuracy.

4. Autonomy vs. control

Machine independence: As machines gain more autonomy, there's a delicate balance between allowing them to operate efficiently and ensuring they don't act in ways that might be ethically questionable. Clear boundaries and guidelines are essential.

Human override: There should always be mechanisms in place for human intervention, allowing humans to override machine decisions when necessary. This ensures that ethical and nuanced human judgement remains at the forefront.

5. Transparency in machine operation

Explainability: For stakeholders to trust machine decisions, they must understand how these decisions are made. This means making algorithms and processes transparent and explainable, even if they're complex.

Open algorithms: While proprietary technology might be a competitive advantage, there's growing advocacy for openness in foundational algorithms, especially in sectors that significantly impact human lives, such as healthcare or criminal justice.

6. Job displacement and human worth

Value of human roles: While automation and AI can take over certain tasks, it's ethically vital to ensure that employees don't feel devalued. Efforts should be made to transition employees into new roles where their human skills – creativity, empathy, strategic thinking – are celebrated and utilised.

Reskilling and education: Companies have an ethical responsibility to aid employees impacted by automation in terms of reskilling, training, and helping them transition to new roles.

7. Long-term impacts and sustainability

Environmental ethics: The environmental footprint of vast computational centres can't be ignored. Organisations need to consider sustainable practices, from energy usage to e-waste management.

Future forecasting: As organisations design their collaborative workforces, they should consider the long-term ethical implications, forecasting how decisions made today might impact society, culture, and individuals in the future.

In essence, the marriage of humans and machines, while promising, is fraught with ethical intricacies. It's up to organisations to weave an ethical fabric into the heart of their collaborative endeavours, ensuring that as we step into the future, we do so with conscience, responsibility, and a deep respect for both human and machine agents in the equation.

ENHANCING DECISION-MAKING THROUGH COLLABORATION

The power of human–machine collaboration comes sharply into focus when we address decision-making. Traditional decision-making frameworks often rely heavily on human intuition, experience, and sometimes even instinct. With the advent of technology, particularly AI and ML, there is now an unprecedented opportunity to merge the computational strengths of machines with the cognitive and emotional nuances of human judgement. This blend has the potential to revolutionise how decisions are made across all sectors and scales. In this section, we explore the different facets of enhanced decision-making through collaboration.

1. Data-driven insight generation

Empirical foundation: Machines, with their ability to process vast datasets quickly, can provide empirical insights that might be missed by human analysts. These insights provide a solid foundation upon which human experts can base their decisions.

Predictive analysis: Advanced algorithms can predict future trends or outcomes based on historical data. This predictive power, when coupled with human intuition and contextual understanding, can help in proactive decision-making.

2. Augmented expertise

Expert systems: These are AI programs that mimic human expertise in specific fields. By collaborating with such systems, professionals can amplify their domain knowledge, benefiting from machine-generated suggestions while retaining final judgement.

Knowledge repositories: Advanced knowledge systems can store and retrieve domain-specific information efficiently, aiding human experts in making well-informed decisions.

3. Real-time decision support

Dynamic environments: In situations that demand real-time decisions, like stock trading or emergency responses, machines can offer instantaneous data processing, laying out potential scenarios for human decision-makers to act upon swiftly.

Monitoring and alerts: Machines can continuously monitor complex systems and alert human overseers to anomalies, ensuring timely intervention and decisions.

4. Multidimensional scenario analysis

Simulation and modelling: Machines can simulate myriad scenarios based on different variables. Such simulations offer decision-makers a holistic view of possible outcomes, enabling them to choose the most optimal path.

Risk assessment: By analysing vast datasets and considering various factors, machines can help in quantifying risks associated with different decisions, allowing humans to make choices that align with organisational risk appetites.

5. Personalised decision-making

Consumer-centric models: In areas like healthcare or marketing, machines can analyse individual-specific data to offer personalised solutions or recommendations. Human professionals can then tailor these machine suggestions further, based on nuanced understanding or direct interactions.

6. Continuous feedback loop

Iterative learning: Decisions, once made, can be fed back into ML models, which can then learn from the outcomes. This iterative learning ensures that decision-making processes are continuously refined over time.

Adaptive algorithms: Machines can adapt based on new data or the outcomes of past decisions, ensuring that their recommendations are always evolving and improving.

7. Collective intelligence and crowdsourcing

Harnessing collective insights: Machines can aggregate and process inputs from a diverse range of sources, from experts to the general populace. This collective intelligence can be invaluable in decisions that benefit from a wide range of perspectives.

8. Overcoming cognitive biases

Neutral processing: While humans sometimes suffer from cognitive biases, machines process data neutrally. By leveraging this, decision-makers can ensure that their choices are not inadvertently swayed by biases or preconceptions.

In conclusion, the fusion of human expertise with machine precision promises a paradigm shift in decision-making efficacy. It is a blend of the emotional intelligence, contextual understanding, and expertise of humans with the data-processing prowess, neutrality, and predictive capabilities of machines. As organisations navigate complex landscapes, this collaborative approach to decision-making stands as a beacon, guiding the way to more informed, timely, and impactful choices.

NURTURING CREATIVITY AND INNOVATION

The emergence of advanced technologies, particularly AI, has raised intriguing questions about the future of creativity and innovation. Can machines be creative? How do humans maintain their creative edge in an era dominated by algorithms? Most importantly, how can the collaborative spirit between humans and machines lead to unprecedented innovation? The answers lie in understanding the unique strengths of both entities and creating an environment where they can synergise effectively.

1. Defining creativity and innovation in the collaborative context

Complementary forces: While machines can process vast amounts of information and identify patterns beyond human comprehension, true creativity often stems from intuition, diverse experiences, emotional intelligence, and cultural contexts. The future of innovation is not about humans competing with machines but collaborating with them.

2. Ideation boosted by technology

Brainstorming with data: Algorithms can process countless data points to suggest possible solutions or directions. By introducing these machine-generated ideas into brainstorming sessions, humans can gain fresh perspectives and insights.

Simulation and visualisation: Advanced graphics, AR, and VR can help innovators visualise complex concepts, experiment with designs in virtual environments, and fast-track the prototyping phase.

3. Fostering a culture of experimentation

Rapid prototyping: With the aid of machines, ideas can be quickly turned into prototypes, allowing for faster feedback and iteration. This rapid prototyping environment encourages risk-taking and experimentation.

Adaptive learning systems: These systems can simulate the outcomes of various innovative ideas, providing immediate feedback and allowing for swift course correction.

4. Encouraging diverse thought and interdisciplinary collaboration

Cross-pollination of ideas: Machines can introduce insights from one domain to another, leading to interdisciplinary innovations. For instance, a solution in computational biology might inspire innovations in data storage.

Global collaboration platforms: Digital platforms can bring together diverse thinkers from across the globe, creating a melting pot of cultures, perspectives, and expertise. This diversity is a potent catalyst for groundbreaking innovations.

5. The role of machines in artistic creation

Algorithmic art and music: Machines can generate art and music based on certain algorithms, providing artists with novel elements to incorporate into their creations.

Augmented design: Designers and artists can use technology to augment their work, whether it's through intricate patterns generated by algorithms or sculptures modelled using 3D printing.

6. Instilling an ethos of lifelong learning

Continuous skill upgradation: As technology evolves, professionals must continuously upgrade their skills. Platforms powered by AI can offer personalised learning pathways, ensuring that learners are always at the forefront of their fields.

Mentorship and coaching: AI-driven coaching tools can provide instant feedback, helping learners refine their creative processes and hone their innovative thinking.

7. Spaces for reflection and mindfulness

Digital detox zones: Ironically, in a digital-first world, there's a growing understanding of the need for spaces devoid of technology. Such spaces allow for deep reflection, a crucial component of the creative process.

Mindfulness tools: While technology can sometimes be overwhelming, there are also digital tools designed to promote mindfulness, focus, and mental wellbeing – all crucial for nurturing creativity.

In the unfolding narrative of human–machine collaboration, creativity and innovation hold a special place. Machines don't aim to replace human creativity but amplify it. By understanding the symbiotic relationship between human intuition and machine precision, organisations can foster an environment where groundbreaking innovations become the norm rather than the exception. The future is not just about intelligent machines but about the heightened potential of human genius when augmented by technology.

PREPARING FOR THE FUTURE: CONTINUOUS EVOLUTION

In the rapidly advancing landscape of human–machine collaboration, organisations must remain proactive rather than reactive. The mesh of advanced technology with human capabilities is not a static phenomenon; it's continuously evolving. As we stand on the cusp of this transformative era, it's paramount for businesses to foster an ethos of ongoing evolution, ensuring they remain agile, relevant, and competitive.

1. Embracing change as the only constant

Organisational fluidity: Traditional hierarchical structures will need to be re-evaluated. An adaptive organisational model, where teams can be quickly formed, modified, and disbanded based on project requirements, can be more conducive to the fast-paced digital era.

Feedback loops: Implementing real-time feedback mechanisms, informed by both human insights and machine analytics, can ensure that strategies and processes are continually refined to meet evolving challenges.

2. Investing in lifelong learning and training

Dynamic learning platforms: Given the rapid technological advancements, traditional training modules can quickly become obsolete. Organisations should invest in dynamic learning platforms that update their curriculum in real time, based on the latest industry trends and technological innovations.

Human–ML synergy: Just as humans need to understand machines better, machines, especially AI, benefit from continuous learning. Implement systems where both humans and machines learn in tandem, adapting to each other's strengths and limitations.

3. Fostering an environment of experimentation

Innovation labs: Create dedicated spaces or labs where teams can experiment with new ideas without the pressure of immediate commercial viability. These labs, equipped with the latest tech tools, can be the birthplaces of groundbreaking solutions.

Risk tolerance: While it's crucial to manage and mitigate risks, organisations should also understand that innovation often requires stepping into the unknown. Cultivate a culture where calculated risks in the pursuit of innovation are not just tolerated but celebrated.

4. Ensuring technological scalability

Modular tech infrastructure: Instead of monolithic tech systems, adopt modular architectures. This allows for smoother integrations of new technologies and ensures that the organisation remains tech-agnostic, able to shift to the best platforms as they emerge.

Future-proofing through R&D: Allocate resources for R&D, focusing on both immediate industry needs and blue-sky solutions that might define the future.

5. Engaging with external innovation ecosystems

Collaborations and partnerships: Form alliances with startups, academic institutions, and research bodies. These entities often operate at the forefront of innovation, and partnerships can lead to mutually beneficial knowledge exchanges.

Staying attuned to global trends: In the digital age, disruption in one part of the world can quickly ripple across the globe. Maintain a global perspective, understanding and adapting to international technological and market trends.

6. Ethical and sustainable evolution

Guided progress: While speed is of the essence, the direction is crucial. Ensure that the pursuit of technological evolution aligns with ethical considerations and promotes sustainability.

Inclusive growth: As organisations evolve, they should ensure that the benefits of technological advancements are equitably distributed, leading to holistic and inclusive growth.

The future is not a distant horizon but an ongoing journey. By embedding a spirit of continuous evolution, organisations can navigate the intricate dance of human–machine collaboration, harnessing its vast potential while shaping a future that reflects our shared aspirations and values. The playbook for tomorrow is written today, and it demands vigilance, adaptability, and a relentless commitment to growth and innovation.

A VISION OF COHESIVE COEXISTENCE

As we stand at the crossroads of the human–machine epoch, it becomes increasingly apparent that the future isn't about choosing between human intuition and machine efficiency, but about leveraging the inherent strengths of both. This chapter, from its introduction to its intricate details, paints a picture of not just collaboration, but cohesive coexistence – a synergy where both entities elevate each other to unprecedented heights.

The journey of human progress has been marked by our ability to use tools, and today's sophisticated technologies are the extensions of this ancient tradition. However, unlike any other time in history, we now have the means to create tools that can think, learn, and, in many respects, evolve. This dynamic shift presents both unparalleled opportunities and intricate challenges.

The myriad discussions and recommendations laid out in this chapter all boil down to one central theme: balance. Whether we're weighing the ethical considerations, nurturing creativity, or preparing for continuous evolution, the equilibrium between human aspirations and machine capabilities is paramount. This balance ensures that we neither lose our human essence in the relentless march of technology nor hold back technological progress due to unfounded fears or inertia.

However, achieving this cohesive coexistence isn't a passive outcome; it requires intentional action. It means fostering a culture that values continuous learning, celebrates innovation, and understands that mistakes, when made in the spirit of exploration, are stepping stones to progress. It means creating environments where people feel empowered to collaborate with machines, understanding that they are not competitors but collaborators.

Moreover, the vision of cohesive coexistence goes beyond just businesses and organisations. It's a clarion call for policymakers, educators, community leaders, and every individual. The digital age doesn't discriminate between sectors or professions; its ripple effects touch every aspect of our lives.

As we conclude this chapter and reflect upon the intricate dance of human–machine collaboration, let's remember that our ultimate aim isn't efficiency or profitability alone. It's about crafting a world where technology enhances human potential, where machines are reflections of our best selves, and where the digital realm is imbued with our shared values and aspirations.

In this era of cohesive coexistence, the narrative isn't about humans versus machines but humans *with* machines, charting a course for a future that's brighter, more inclusive, and filled with boundless possibilities.

GLOBAL BEST PRACTICE: DELOITTE'S FRAMEWORK FOR STRENGTHENING THE BONDS OF HUMAN AND MACHINE COLLABORATION

In Deloitte's insightful article, 'Strengthening the bonds of human and machine collaboration', (Deloitte Insights), the evolving dynamics between humans and AI in the workplace are intricately explored. The analysis paints a picture of a rapidly changing landscape, where the promise of innovation is both exciting and laden with challenges. At the onset, Deloitte acknowledges the hurdles faced in integrating AI into daily operations. Instances such as Uber drivers circumventing AI algorithms or call centre reps grappling with AI handling rudimentary queries showcase the intricate balance required to maintain human job satisfaction.

The spectrum of collaboration is vast, ranging from AI assisting in directed tasks to more sophisticated, interactive roles where AI acts as an equal teammate. Advanced language models like OpenAI's GPT-3 and Google's LaMDA exemplify the potential of AI in fostering enhanced human–AI dialogues, responding adeptly to human cues. However, the proliferation of AI does introduce complexities to traditional roles, potentially threatening entry-level jobs and amplifying the need for upskilling.

A poignant aspect Deloitte delves into is the socio-psychological impact of AI. With AI potentially acting as supervisors, the workplace could become more regimented, possibly diminishing worker autonomy and engagement. Moreover, consistent interaction with AI might lead to feelings of isolation among employees, raising questions about identity in a machine-dominated environment. The remedy, as proposed, lies in ensuring human-centric AI design, bolstering social connections, and drafting clear protocols for AI–human interactions.

To navigate this transformative era, Deloitte offers the below framework and guiding principles. These include designating leaders to oversee collaboration optimisation, reshaping workforce strategies, and gearing up for a perpetually evolving employment landscape. The article's conclusion is a clarion call for organisations to wholeheartedly adopt and mould human–machine collaborations, ensuring a symbiotic relationship that benefits both the business landscape and its invaluable human assets.

FIGURE 6. DELOITTE INSIGHTS

The many ways humans can friend a machine at work

	Machines as supervisors	Machines as teammates	Machines as subordinates
Suggest and iterate: Machines make real-time suggestions that humans consider, with a frequent and iterative dialogue and loop between the two		The personal coach / The muse	The collaborative decision-maker
Sequence: Humans and machines perform work separately and in sequential order, but check on one another's work	The prioritizer		The first pass at a task / The triage nurse
Replicate: Machines replicate human work with human oversight as needed	The supervisor		The doppelganger / The subordinate

Type of interaction with AI

Type of authority of AI

Type of collaboration	Definition
The supervisor	An algorithm allocates tasks-for example, a ridesharing company that uses AI to dispatch rides to drivers who have a few seconds to accept or reject a ride request without knowing the destination or fare. Performance and pay are determined by AI. An algorithm also decides when morale-boosting motivational messages are needed.
The prioritizer	An AI algorithm addresses a list of tasks-sales leads to be pursued, medical problems to solve, fundraising opportunities to follow up on-and ranks them in terms of their importance or potential value. The human worker then pursues them in order, sometimes with suggestions from the machine about how to do so.
The personal coach	AI discovers the human worker's strengths and opportunities for improvement on a specific task (such as a telephone or video sales call), resulting in continuous engagement with AI to improve the human's performance.
The muse	Multiple creative suggestions are prompted by a human, output by a machine, and iterated in an ongoing collaboration. Examples include design suggestions based on architect prompts and AI-driven generative design.
The collaborative decision-maker	Complex decisions, such as medical diagnoses, are made in a dialogue between AI and humans, and where AI can improve decisions by enumerating available options, helping people weigh them objectively, and suggesting the highest probability of successful action.
First pass at a task	A machine performs the first pass at a task-a life insurance application, a medical-coding categorization, an analysis of an MRI scan-and makes a preliminary decision or judgement. The human worker reviews the analysis and determines if it is correct. The order of this sequence could also be reversed.
The triage nurse	AI assesses the problem (medical symptoms, for example) and decides whether a human consultation is necessary; if not, it dispenses advice to address the relatively minor problem.
The doppelganger	Machines learn from a human or group of humans to mimic their behaviors and decisions, so that the human(s) can be replicated digitally.
The subordinate	AI systems perform menial, structured tasks (like extracting key data from documents or faxes) under human supervision and review.

Deloitte Insights | deloitte.com/insights

This framework by Deloitte serves as a compelling example of a global best practice, reminding us of the intricate dance between technology and humanity in shaping the future of work.

GLOBAL BEST PRACTICE: EXAMPLES OF EFFECTIVE HUMAN–MACHINE COLLABORATION

1. Google's DeepMind and healthcare professionals

- Project: Developed AI for spotting eye diseases in scans.
- Collaboration: Working with Moorfields Eye Hospital to analyse retinal scans.

2. IBM's Watson and oncologists

- Project: Watson for Oncology assists doctors in identifying cancer treatments.
- Collaboration: Oncologists use Watson's information for patient care decisions.

3. Microsoft's Hanover Project

- Project: Developed ML tools for cancer research.
- Collaboration: Researchers and doctors apply AI insights in experimental treatments.

4. Facebook's content moderation

- Project: Uses AI tools to detect and remove harmful content.
- Collaboration: Human moderators review flagged content for context.

5. Amazon's fulfilment centres

- Project: Employs robots for transporting goods.
- Collaboration: Human employees handle quality control and dexterous tasks.

6. Apple's Siri and user interface

- Project: Siri uses AI to interpret user commands.
- Collaboration: Developers and linguists train Siri and refine its responses.

7. Tesla's Autopilot

- Project: Advanced driver-assistance system in Tesla vehicles.
- Collaboration: Requires active supervision by a human driver.

8. Healthcare: Radiology and AI imaging

- Project: AI aids radiologists in identifying abnormalities in medical scans.

- Collaboration: Radiologists review AI results for accurate diagnoses.

9. Agriculture: Precision farming

- Project: Drones with AI scan fields for agricultural insights.
- Collaboration: Farmers combine AI data with their expertise for decisions.

10. Finance: Fraud detection

- Project: AI detects irregularities in transaction patterns.
- Collaboration: Human investigators review flagged transactions.

11. Retail: Customer service chatbot

- Project: Chatbots answer customer queries.
- Collaboration: Human representatives handle complex issues.

12. Manufacturing: Collaborative robots (cobots)

- Project: Cobots assist human workers in various tasks.
- Collaboration: Human workers oversee and intervene as needed.

13. Entertainment: Script and music generation

- Project: AI generates music and suggests script changes.
- Collaboration: Artists use AI-generated content as inspiration.

14. Energy: Predictive maintenance

- Project: AI analyses equipment data for predictive maintenance.
- Collaboration: Maintenance crews use AI data for informed decisions.

15. Journalism: Automated reporting

- Project: AI automates certain news article writing.
- Collaboration: Journalists add context and analysis to auto-generated content.

Transitioning from Chapter 10, which explored the intricate dynamics between human creativity and machine efficiency, to Chapter 11 – Redefining Roles and Reskilling, we shift our focus to the practical implications of this synergy on the workforce. This chapter delves into how the integration of humans and machines alters existing job roles and creates a need for significant reskilling and upskilling within organisations.

REDEFINING ROLES AND RESKILLING

The reshaping of the modern workforce in the digital era brings forth both challenges and opportunities. As traditional roles undergo transformation with automation taking over manual tasks, new and unprecedented roles are emerging. This dynamic landscape necessitates a proactive approach to reskilling, ensuring employees aren't just reactive to change but are prepared to harness it. In this chapter, we will look at the intricacies and considerations of job transformations and provide actionable strategies for organisations to empower their workforce with the skills they'll need to thrive in the future.

EMBRACING THE ERA OF ROLE REDEFINITION

The winds of change have been sweeping through industries with increasing intensity. As digitalisation and automation take root, we stand on the cusp of a transformative wave. It's evident that the nature of work as we know it is undergoing a profound metamorphosis.

A historical perspective

Historically, every major industrial revolution has necessitated a re-evaluation of roles and skillsets. The transition from agrarian societies to industrial ones saw people shifting from farms to factories. Similarly, the rise of the internet in the late 20th century sparked a digital revolution that created new avenues of work. Each shift has led to anxieties about obsolescence, but also paved the way for innovation and growth.

The current landscape

Today, the Fourth Industrial Revolution, powered by technologies like AI, blockchain, and the IoT, is reshaping industries. Routine tasks, once the backbone of many job roles, are becoming automated. Customer service bots, automated financial algorithms, and AI-driven diagnostics in healthcare are just a few examples of the change.

Yet, while automation is streamlining certain job functions, it's concurrently opening doors to roles that were previously unimaginable. Think of positions like AI ethicists, digital transformation specialists, or even AR experience designers. These are roles born out of the confluence of human creativity and technological advancement.

The dual challenge

Organisations are now faced with a dual challenge. First, there's the task of identifying which roles are becoming redundant or evolving due to technological intervention. Then, there's the equally crucial task of foreseeing emerging roles and preparing the workforce to step into these new shoes.

But role redefinition isn't just about charting out job descriptions; it's about recognising that the very essence of many jobs is becoming more fluid and collaborative. Jobs of the future might not fit neatly into boxes or departments but could be interdisciplinary, project-based, and dynamically responsive to industry needs.

Beyond technical skills

While much of the focus is on the technical skills required for the digital age, such as coding or data analytics, the soft skills – like adaptability, critical thinking, and emotional intelligence – are gaining unprecedented importance. As machines take over routine tasks, human workers will be valued more for their ability to solve complex problems, lead teams, and innovate – qualities that machines are far from replicating.

Embracing the era of role redefinition requires vision, resilience, and a commitment to continuous learning.

Organisations that proactively address these shifts, fostering a culture of adaptability and lifelong learning, are poised to not only survive but thrive in this new age. In the subsequent sections, we will take a closer look at strategies and best practices to navigate this transformative landscape.

THE IMPETUS FOR CHANGE

At the heart of the seismic shifts in the world of work lies a series of catalysts driving the need for redefined roles and reskilling. These drivers are multifaceted, ranging from technological breakthroughs to socioeconomic factors. Recognising and understanding them is the first step in charting a clear path forward for organisations and their workforces.

Technological evolution

Digital revolution: The digital revolution, characterised by the rise of the internet, smartphones, and ubiquitous connectivity, has fundamentally changed how we communicate, work, and live. Tasks that were manual and time-consuming have been transformed by software and automation tools.

AI and automation: The astounding pace of advancements in AI and ML has enabled automation at an unprecedented scale. Jobs that revolved around data analysis, repetitive tasks, and even certain decision-making processes are now being augmented or replaced by intelligent algorithms.

Emerging technologies: Beyond AI, technologies like block-chain, AR and VR, and IoT are opening new horizons for businesses, leading to the creation of niche roles specialised in harnessing the potential of these technologies.

Socioeconomic shifts

Globalisation: In an interconnected world, organisations are tapping into global talent pools, leading to a confluence of diverse skills and cultural perspectives. This necessitates a workforce adept in cross-cultural communication and collaboration.

Changing workforce demographics: As millennials and gen Z become dominant workforce demographics, there's a push towards flexible working models, purpose-driven roles, and a blend of technical and soft skills.

Sustainability and ethical considerations: Increasingly, businesses are being held accountable for their societal and environmental impact. This has led to the rise of roles focusing on sustainability initiatives, ethical AI implementation, and corporate social responsibility.

Organisational dynamics

Agile and lean methodologies: Modern organisations are gravitating towards agile and lean approaches, favouring iterative processes and cross-functional teams over traditional hierarchical structures. This has a ripple effect on job roles, emphasising adaptability and multidisciplinary knowledge.

Customer-centricity: The modern consumer demands personalised experiences, pushing businesses to adopt roles that prioritise user experience, customer journey mapping, and data-driven insights.

The urgency of adaptation

While change is a constant, the velocity and magnitude of the current changes are unparalleled. The impetus for change isn't just about staying competitive; it's about survival. Organisations that fail to recognise and act on these catalysts risk obsolescence.

The impetus for change is fuelled by a confluence of technological, socioeconomic, and organisational factors. Recognising them is crucial, but acting on them with foresight and agility will define the success stories of the future. The following sections will explore how organisations can strategically navigate this landscape, ensuring their workforce is not just prepared but empowered for the challenges and opportunities that lie ahead.

IDENTIFYING VULNERABLE ROLES

In the rapidly evolving landscape of the digital era, certain job roles face the risk of becoming redundant or significantly altered due to advancements in technology. Understanding which roles are vulnerable is the first step toward proactive planning and ensuring that the workforce remains agile and relevant. This section delves into the process and importance of identifying these roles and offers insights on how organisations can approach this challenge.

Understanding vulnerability in the context of roles

The term 'vulnerable' in the context of job roles doesn't necessarily denote negativity. Instead, it signifies roles that are prone to change or evolution due to technological advancements. Vulnerable roles can be classified into two primary categories:

1. Roles at risk of automation: These are roles that consist of repetitive tasks or functions that can be easily codified. As automation technologies become more sophisticated, these tasks can be executed more efficiently by machines.

2. Roles undergoing transformation: These roles might not disappear entirely but will evolve to integrate more with emerging technologies, requiring new skillsets.

Indicators of vulnerability

Several indicators can signal the vulnerability of a particular role:

1. Repetitiveness: Jobs that involve a high degree of routine and repetition are prime candidates for automation. For instance, data entry tasks or basic administrative functions can often be streamlined with software solutions.

2. Lack of human-centric skills: Roles that don't heavily rely on emotional intelligence, creativity, critical thinking, or human interaction are more susceptible to automation.

3. High error rates: Tasks where human error can have significant repercussions, such as quality control in manufacturing, might be transitioned to machines for increased precision.

4. Rapid technological changes: Jobs in fields where technology is advancing at a breakneck pace might see quick shifts in role requirements.

Methods to identify vulnerable roles

1. Skills and task analysis: By breaking down each role into its constituent tasks and skills, organisations can evaluate which are routine or can be automated.

2. Market research: Observing trends in the industry and understanding where competitors are investing in technology can offer insights into potential areas of vulnerability.

3. Employee feedback: Engaging with employees can provide ground-level insights. They often have a clear understanding of the repetitive or time-consuming aspects of their jobs that can be optimised.

4. Consultation with tech experts: Collaborating with technology consultants or experts can help in understanding upcoming technological innovations that might influence roles.

Addressing the identified vulnerabilities

Once vulnerable roles are identified, it's not a signal to eliminate these jobs but rather an opportunity to evolve and adapt. Reskilling and upskilling become paramount, ensuring that employees in these roles are equipped to transition into the roles of the future, roles that provide more value and satisfaction.

In conclusion, identifying vulnerable roles is not about predicting obsolescence but preparing for transformation. It's a forward-looking approach, ensuring that the organisation and its workforce remain resilient and future-ready in the face of technological advancements.

THE EVOLUTION OF JOBS IN A DIGITAL LANDSCAPE

As we progress further into the digital age, certain job roles, previously deemed as constants, are now undergoing significant evolution. Understanding which roles are on the cusp of this transformative shift is paramount to fostering proactive adaptation. The challenge isn't solely about identifying diminishing roles but also about discerning their potential evolutionary trajectories. This section elucidates these nuances and paints a vision for organisations looking to stay ahead of the curve.

FIGURE 7.

OPERATIONAL ROLES	INSIGHT-DRIVEN ROLES
MONO-SKILLED ROLES	MULTISKILLED ROLES
GENERALIST ROLES	SPECIALIZED ROLES
TECHNOLOGY-ORIENTED ROLES	CREATIVE ROLES

Operational roles morphing into insight-driven capacities

Historically, operational roles have been anchored in routine tasks and regular oversight. But the dawn of automation and sophisticated data analytics is reshaping them:

- Automated data capture: Tasks that once demanded manual data entry or monitoring are swiftly being replaced by real-time data capture mechanisms.

- Insight extraction: Rather than merely managing operations, future roles will demand an ability to sift through data, extracting actionable insights.
- Strategising with data: The operational workforce will increasingly lean into data for strategic decision-making, trend predictions, and efficiency amplifications.

To illustrate this point, consider a factory floor supervisor. While previously engrossed in machinery oversight, they might soon be optimising production workflows based on data analytics insights.

Mono-skilled jobs broadening into multiskilled profiles

The digital realm demands versatility. Mono-skilled jobs, characterised by a singular focus, are expanding their horizons:

- Expanding skillsets: Employees are now being cross-trained, equipping them to straddle multiple functions.
- Functional convergence: A single job role might soon encapsulate responsibilities from diverse domains, resulting in a more comprehensive job blueprint.

Envision a customer service representative. Beyond merely addressing queries, they might soon manage social media feedback and execute basic tech troubleshooting.

The refinement from generalist stances to specialised niches

As the granularity of industry-specific knowledge intensifies, generalist roles are refining into specialised avatars:

- In-depth expertise: While the breadth of knowledge is a generalist's forte, specialists immerse themselves in particular areas, becoming subject-matter authorities.
- Endless curiosity: This transformation from generalist to specialist necessitates an unquenchable thirst for learning and staying abreast of niche developments.

For instance, a marketer with a generalist's perspective might now become an expert focusing solely on facets like data-driven marketing, SEO nuances, or content strategy.

Technology-centric roles pivoting to embrace creativity

With AI and ML becoming adept at handling technologically intensive tasks, humans are returning to their unique forte – creativity:

- Brainstorming innovations: As machines dominate execution, human roles will pivot towards ideation and innovation.
- Emphasising human-centric design: The roles that will lead the future are those that shape technology to align with real human needs, behaviours, and emotions – ensuring solutions resonate on a deeply personal level.

- Fusion of disciplines: Tech professionals will frequently intersect with artists, psychologists, and other creatives, weaving holistic solutions.

A case in point is the software developer's role. Beyond pure coding, they might now collaborate with UX/UI designers or even behavioural scientists, aiming to craft intuitive user experiences.

The digital realm is not about job replacements but rather job evolution. It champions a dynamic reimagining of roles, retraining paradigms, and workforce engagement. By staying attuned to these role evolutions, organisations can sculpt their workforce strategies, ensuring they remain innovative, relevant, and primed for growth in a digital-first world.

RESKILLING: A PROACTIVE APPROACH

In today's rapidly changing business environment, organisations can no longer afford a reactive stance when it comes to talent development. The digital transformation that underpins contemporary industry evolution is not just altering roles but creating entirely new ones. As the previous sections have shown, jobs are evolving at an unprecedented rate. This calls for a proactive approach to talent development – a focus on reskilling.

The imperative of reskilling in a digital age

The pervasive march of automation, AI, and other digital tools is a double-edged sword. While they bring efficiency and innovation, they also necessitate a workforce equipped with new competencies. Reskilling, thus, is not a mere strategy but a business imperative.

Future-proofing the workforce: As roles evolve, there's a risk of skill redundancy. Reskilling ensures employees are always equipped with relevant and future-oriented skills, safeguarding their roles against obsolescence.

Enhancing organisational agility: A workforce that is continually upskilled is agile, ready to adapt to market shifts, and primed to leverage emergent technologies.

Strategies for effective reskilling

1. Skills gap analysis: Begin with a thorough assessment of the existing skillsets within the organisation versus those demanded by your industry's future. This will help in pinpointing specific areas of focus.

2. Blended learning models: Harness a mix of traditional classroom training, e-learning modules, workshops, and hands-on projects. This multifaceted approach ensures comprehensive skill acquisition.

3. Real-world application: Theory without practice is futile. Create opportunities for employees to apply their new skills

in real-world scenarios, aiding in skill consolidation and confidence-building.

4. Partner with educational institutions: Collaborating with universities and training institutions ensures that the reskilling programs are in line with industry demands and leverage the latest educational methodologies.

5. Continuous feedback mechanisms: Reskilling is a continuous journey. Implement feedback loops with employees to understand the effectiveness of training modules and areas for improvement.

6. Foster a culture of lifelong learning: Beyond structured training, encourage employees to adopt a mindset of continuous self-improvement. Platforms like online courses, webinars, and workshops can facilitate this.

Reskilling is not just about equipping employees with a new set of skills. It's about instilling a proactive approach to adaptation, ensuring that as the business landscape morphs, the workforce is not left behind but develops alongside it. By adopting a forward-thinking strategy towards reskilling, organisations not only protect their most valuable assets – their employees – but also ensure sustained competitiveness in a digital-first world.

THE ROLE OF LEADERSHIP IN RESKILLING

In the journey of organisational transformation, leadership plays a pivotal role. When it comes to reskilling initiatives, their influence is even more pronounced. Effective leadership can drive a culture of continuous learning, while also ensuring that reskilling efforts align with broader organisational objectives. Next is an exploration of how leaders can steer the ship of reskilling effectively.

Visionary thinking

Leaders must possess the foresight to anticipate future industry trends and understand the implications these might have on workforce skills. This visionary thinking allows for the early identification of potential skill gaps and the crafting of strategic reskilling programs well in advance.

Prioritising reskilling

For any initiative to gain traction, it must be prioritised at the highest levels. Leaders should position reskilling as a top organisational priority, signalling its importance to all stakeholders. This can manifest in the allocation of resources, time, and attention towards training programs and continuous learning efforts.

Creating an environment of psychological safety

Change can be daunting, and for employees accustomed to certain ways of working, reskilling might be met with resistance or anxiety. Leaders have the responsibility to create an environment of psychological safety where employees feel comfortable embracing new learning opportunities without fear of failure or reprisal.

Collaborative approach

While leaders might set the direction, the process of reskilling is collaborative. Engaging middle management, team leads, and even frontline employees in the decision-making process ensures diverse perspectives are considered, and the training programs developed are well-rounded and effective.

Measuring and celebrating success

It's not enough to simply launch reskilling programs; their efficacy must be measured. Leaders should establish clear metrics of success, track progress, and importantly, celebrate milestones. Recognising and rewarding those who excel in their reskilling journey can serve as motivation for others.

Leading by example

Perhaps the most potent tool in a leader's arsenal is their own actions. By actively participating in continuous learning, seeking feedback, and showcasing their own reskilling journey, leaders can inspire others to follow suit.

Ensuring sustainability

Reskilling is not a one-off initiative but a continuous process. Leaders need to ensure the sustainability of these efforts. This might involve periodic reviews of training programs, staying abreast of emerging industry trends, or establishing partnerships with educational institutions for ongoing curriculum development.

The role of leadership in reskilling transcends mere strategy formulation. It delves into the realms of culture creation, motivation, and continuous support. As organisations navigate the choppy waters of digital transformation, strong, committed leadership can serve as the beacon, guiding the workforce towards a future of growth and adaptability.

Overcoming reskilling challenges

Reskilling, while essential for the modern workforce's adaptability and growth, is not without its hurdles. From resistance to change to resource constraints, organisations often face a slew of challenges when initiating and sustaining reskilling efforts. This section delves into these challenges and offers actionable strategies to overcome them.

1. Resistance to change

Many employees, especially those who have been in a particular role or industry for a long time, might be resistant to the idea of reskilling. This resistance can stem from fear of the unknown, concerns about job security, or simply comfort with the status quo.

Strategy: Open communication is crucial. Engage employees in dialogues about the changing industry landscape, the benefits of acquiring new skills, and the tangible ways in which reskilling can enhance their career trajectory. Make it clear that reskilling is an investment in them and their future.

2. Identifying relevant skills

With the rapid pace of technological advancement and market evolution, pinpointing which skills are most relevant can be a moving target.

Strategy: Instead of solely focusing on hard skills, prioritise foundational skills like critical thinking, adaptability, and problem-solving. Collaborate with industry experts, invest in forecasting tools, and keep a finger on the pulse of market trends to refine skill targets.

3. Resource constraints

For many organisations, especially smaller ones, there might be limited resources (both in terms of time and money) to allocate towards reskilling.

Strategy: Leverage online learning platforms, many of which offer high-quality courses at affordable rates. Additionally, consider collaborative learning approaches, such as mentorship programs or peer-led workshops, which can be cost-effective and foster team cohesion.

4. Measuring reskilling ROI

Determining the ROI for reskilling initiatives can be complex, especially in the short term.

Strategy: Shift the perspective from immediate monetary returns to long-term value propositions like employee retention, increased adaptability, and enhanced productivity. Use

qualitative feedback, engagement metrics, and skill application instances as ROI indicators.

5. Time constraints

Employees, often swamped with their daily tasks, might feel
they lack the time for reskilling efforts.

Strategy: Integrate learning into daily workflows. This could
be in the form of bite-sized learning modules, dedicated
'learning hours' each week, or integrating real-world projects
that allow for on-the-job skill development.

6. Keeping momentum

Starting a reskilling initiative with enthusiasm is one thing,
but maintaining momentum over time is another.

Strategy: Regularly update the curriculum to keep it relevant
and engaging. Celebrate milestones, share success stories,
and continuously reinforce the long-term benefits of reskilling. Consider gamifying the learning process to enhance
engagement.

7. Balancing immediate needs with future goals

Organisations may struggle with the dichotomy of addressing current operational requirements while preparing for
future skill needs.

Strategy: Adopt a phased approach to reskilling. While immediate skill gaps are addressed as a priority, allocate resources
and time for long-term skill development in parallel.

In conclusion, while the path to comprehensive reskilling may be riddled with obstacles, with strategic planning, clear communication, and a commitment to continuous learning, these challenges can be surmounted. Overcoming these hurdles not only equips organisations with a future-ready workforce but also demonstrates a genuine commitment to employee growth and wellbeing.

FOSTERING A CULTURE OF CONTINUOUS LEARNING

As the boundaries of knowledge and technology constantly expand, it becomes ever more essential for organisations to cultivate an environment that not only values learning but also embeds it into the very fabric of its culture. An ethos of continuous learning isn't just about formal training or acquiring new skills; it's about nurturing curiosity, adaptability, and an unceasing quest for improvement. Here's how organisations can foster such a culture:

1. Lead by example

Top leadership and management should actively participate in learning programs, showcasing their commitment to personal growth. When employees see their leaders valuing and partaking in continuous learning, it sets a powerful precedent.

2. Personalise learning pathways

Recognise that each individual has a unique learning style and pace. Offering personalised learning pathways – be it through modular online courses, interactive workshops, or hands-on training – ensures that employees can learn in a manner most effective for them.

3. Incorporate learning into daily tasks

Continuous learning shouldn't be seen as an additional task but rather as an integral part of daily operations. Encourage employees to set aside dedicated 'learning breaks', explore new tools relevant to their tasks, or engage in knowledge-sharing sessions.

4. Recognise and reward learning

Establish systems to acknowledge and reward employees who are proactive in their learning endeavours. This could be through certifications, badges, monetary incentives, or even opportunities to lead new projects based on their recently acquired knowledge.

5. Encourage cross-functional learning

Breaking silos and encouraging departments to learn from one another can lead to holistic skill development. Rotate employees between different functions or set up interdisciplinary projects to foster a broader understanding of the organisation.

6. Create safe spaces for experimentation

Learning often comes from trying, failing, and iterating. Create environments where employees feel safe to test new ideas, make mistakes, and learn from them without the fear of repercussions.

7. Leverage technology

Utilise digital platforms, AI-driven tools, and online repositories to offer a diverse range of learning resources. This allows employees to access and engage with content that's most relevant to them, any time and anywhere.

8. Foster mentorship and peer learning

While formal training is valuable, a lot can be learnt from peers and mentors. Setting up mentorship programs, peer-led workshops, or even informal 'knowledge cafes' can facilitate rich exchanges of insights and experiences.

9. Open channels for feedback

Ensure that there are avenues for employees to provide feedback on learning programs and resources. This helps refine the offerings and empowers employees by involving them in the process.

10. Instil a growth mindset

Promote the belief that abilities and intelligence can be developed through dedication and hard work. When employees believe they can grow and evolve, they're more likely to invest time in learning and face challenges with resilience.

Building a culture of continuous learning is a journey, not a destination. It requires consistent effort, adaptability, and a commitment from every tier of the organisation. But the rewards – a nimble, future-ready workforce; increased innovation; and sustained competitive advantage – make it an endeavour worth pursuing.

CASE STUDIES: SUCCESSFUL RESKILLING INITIATIVES

Across the globe, organisations have recognised the importance of reskilling and have taken proactive measures to ensure their workforce remains agile and equipped for the evolving demands of the industry. In this section, we'll explore a few notable case studies that showcase successful reskilling initiatives.

1. General Assembly & L'Oréal's digital upskilling

Beauty giant L'Oréal partnered with education provider General Assembly to upskill their employees in digital competencies. This collaboration sought to address the digital transformation challenges in the beauty industry. Over 1,000 employees went through rigorous training sessions that covered everything from digital marketing and e-commerce strategies to data analytics. The initiative both bolstered L'Oréal's digital prowess and underscored the company's commitment to the growth of its employees.

2. Amazon's Upskilling 2025 pledge

Aware of the potential displacement automation could bring, Amazon committed US$700 million to upskill 100,000 of its workers by 2025. This commitment, known as the Upskilling 2025 pledge, offers various training programs, from software engineering courses for tech-savvy employees to training in nursing for those interested in medical careers. Recognising that the jobs of tomorrow require a diverse skillset, Amazon's programs aim to prepare its workforce for both internal promotions and external career changes.

3. JPMorganChase & Co's New Skills at Work initiative

This financial institution launched a US$350 million global initiative, New Skills at Work, with a focus on preparing people for the future of work. Concentrating on industries like healthcare and advanced manufacturing, the initiative aims to identify and close the skill gaps. By collaborating with educational institutions and tech employers, JPMorgan is focusing on creating pathways to well-paying careers, all while ensuring its workforce remains adaptive and resilient.

4. Siemens' dual education system

Drawing inspiration from the German model of vocational training, Siemens introduced a dual education system in various locations, including the United States. This approach combines theoretical coursework with hands-on training in the company's plants and innovation hubs. By providing apprenticeships in areas like mechatronics, Siemens ensures that students get the skills that are directly applicable to their jobs, resulting in a workforce that is both knowledgeable and practical.

These case studies exemplify that effective reskilling isn't just about introducing new training programs but about creating a comprehensive ecosystem of continuous learning. Whether it's by forging partnerships with educational institutions, leveraging technology, or dedicating substantial resources, these organisations underscore the importance of proactive reskilling in today's dynamic world.

GLOBAL BEST PRACTICE: AT&T'S FUTURE-READY INITIATIVE – A BLUEPRINT FOR GLOBAL DIGITAL RESKILLING EXCELLENCE

In a world of rapid technological evolution, maintaining a future-ready workforce has become a paramount concern for organisations. This case study explores how AT&T, a telecommunications giant, addressed this challenge head-on through its 'Future Ready' initiative, setting a benchmark for digital reskilling practices on a global scale.

Background

Company profile
AT&T is a leading telecommunications and media conglomerate with a vast employee base of approximately 250,000 individuals.

Challenges
AT&T faced a pivotal challenge: Nearly half of its workforce lacked the skills required to meet the company's

changing technological demands. With the threat of workforce obsolescence looming, AT&T embarked on an ambitious journey to transform its employees into digital-savvy professionals.

Initiative overview

AT&T's Future Ready initiative: Launched as a multi-year, billion-dollar campaign, the Future Ready initiative aimed to reskill its workforce comprehensively and proactively. The key components of this initiative were as follows:

1. Online courses

AT&T recognised the need for scalable and accessible learning. They partnered with leading online education platforms to offer a wide array of courses. These courses covered topics ranging from emerging technologies to soft skills required in the digital age.

2. Collaborations with universities

To bring academic rigor into its reskilling efforts, AT&T formed strategic partnerships with renowned universities. These collaborations resulted in customised programs tailored to AT&T's specific needs, blending academic expertise with practical industry knowledge.

3. Internal education platform

AT&T developed an internal education platform, accessible to all employees. This platform featured self-assessment tools to identify skill gaps, recommend personalised coursework, and track progress. It became a hub for continuous learning and development.

4. Subsidised degree programs

Recognising the long-term value of formal education, AT&T introduced subsidised degree programs. Employees who aspired to earn degrees in fields relevant to their roles received financial support from the company. This initiative encouraged employees to pursue higher education while working.

5. Internal apprenticeship programs

Post-reskilling, AT&T launched internal apprenticeship programs. These programs provided a practical, hands-on learning experience for employees to apply their newly acquired skills in real-world scenarios. It bridged the gap between theory and practice, ensuring that reskilled employees were job-ready.

Execution

The Future Ready initiative was executed with precision and inclusivity:

1. Employee engagement

AT&T made reskilling a priority for every employee, emphasising that learning was a lifelong journey. They organised awareness campaigns, workshops, and town hall meetings to engage and inspire the workforce.

2. Managerial support

Managers were actively involved in identifying skill gaps within their teams and encouraging employees to take advantage of the reskilling opportunities. Performance evaluations included an emphasis on digital competencies.

3. Flexibility

Recognising the need to balance work and learning, AT&T offered flexible schedules and incentives for employees to dedicate time to upskilling.

Outcomes

The Future Ready initiative bore impressive results:

1. Enhanced workforce competence

Over the course of the initiative, AT&T's workforce transformed into a digitally proficient and adaptable group. Skill gaps were significantly reduced, ensuring that employees were equipped to meet the evolving demands of the company.

2. Business agility

With a future-ready workforce, AT&T became more agile in adopting new technologies and responding to market changes swiftly. This translated into a competitive edge in the telecommunications industry.

3. Employee retention

The initiative not only upskilled the workforce but also boosted employee morale and job satisfaction. Employees appreciated the investment in their development, leading to improved retention rates.

4. Industry leadership

AT&T's Future Ready initiative set a benchmark in the telecommunications industry and became a reference point for digital reskilling efforts globally.

AT&T's Future Ready initiative serves as a shining example of digital reskilling excellence on a global scale. By combining online courses, academic collaborations, a robust internal education platform, subsidised degree programs, and internal apprenticeship initiatives, AT&T transformed its workforce into a future-ready powerhouse, ensuring its continued success in a rapidly changing digital landscape. This case study demonstrates that with vision, commitment, and strategic planning, organisations can thrive in the face of technological disruption by investing in their most valuable asset: their people.

AT&T's reskilling journey underscores the importance of proactive adaptation. In an era where change is the only constant, their approach serves as a blueprint for other organisations aiming to remain relevant and competitive.

In Chapter 11, we explored the dynamic changes in job roles and the growing need for continuous skill development to stay relevant in the rapidly evolving workplace. We recognised that as traditional roles evolve and new roles emerge, a strategic approach to employee development is crucial. Next, in Chapter 12, we build on this understanding by presenting concrete reskilling frameworks that organisations can implement.

RESKILLING FRAMEWORKS

In the evolving digital landscape, where technological advancements and shifting market dynamics render certain skills obsolete while creating demand for new competencies, organisations face the critical challenge of ensuring their workforce remains agile, skilled, and prepared for the future. Building on the insights from Chapter 10, this chapter explores actionable reskilling frameworks that organisations can adopt to navigate this transformative era successfully. These frameworks are designed to be adaptable, allowing for customisation based on specific industry needs, organisational culture, and workforce demographics.

STRATEGIC RESKILLING FRAMEWORK

1. Assessment and identification of skill gaps

- Comprehensive skills audit: Conduct a thorough analysis of current workforce capabilities versus future skill requirements, considering technological trends and strategic business objectives.

- Employee surveys and feedback: Leverage surveys and direct feedback to understand employee aspirations, perceived skill gaps, and areas of interest for professional development.

2. Development of reskilling pathways

- Customised learning journeys: Based on the skills audit, create personalised learning paths for employees, incorporating both digital and soft skills relevant to future organisational needs.
- Blended learning approaches: Use a mix of e-learning, workshops, on-the-job training, and mentoring to cater to diverse learning preferences and facilitate practical application of new skills.

3. Partnership and collaboration

- Collaboration with educational institutions: Develop partnerships with universities and online education platforms to access cutting-edge curriculum and resources.
- Industry consortiums: Join or create consortiums with other organisations to share best practices and learning resources, and even co-develop industry-specific training programs.

4. Implementation and integration

- Learning in the flow of work: Integrate reskilling initiatives into daily work activities, making learning an integral part of the employee's job rather than an additional task.
- Project-based learning: Encourage employees to apply new skills on real projects, providing a safe environment for experimentation and learning from failures.

5. Monitoring, evaluation, and continuous improvement

- Skill application tracking: Implement mechanisms to track the application of new skills in the workplace, linking learning outcomes to performance metrics.
- Continuous feedback loop: Establish a continuous feedback system involving learners, trainers, and managers to gather insights on the effectiveness of reskilling programs and areas for improvement.

6. Culture and leadership support

- Leadership endorsement: Ensure top management actively supports and participates in reskilling initiatives, demonstrating a commitment to continuous learning.

> • Foster a learning culture: Cultivate an organisational culture that values curiosity and continuous improvement, and views reskilling as an ongoing journey rather than a one-time event.

INNOVATIVE RESKILLING TECHNIQUES

1. Gamification: Incorporate game design elements into learning programs to increase engagement, motivation, and retention of knowledge. Interactive challenges and rewards make learning more enjoyable and effective.

2. Microlearning: Leverage short, focused learning modules for easier consumption during breaks or between tasks, making learning more accessible and less overwhelming.

3. Peer learning: Facilitate forums, discussion groups, and peer teaching opportunities, leveraging collective knowledge within the organisation to foster a supportive learning community.

4. VR and AR: Use VR and AR for immersive learning experiences, especially for complex skills or procedures, providing a hands-on approach in a safe, controlled environment.

5. AI-powered personalisation: Use AI to tailor learning content and pacing to individual progress, preferences,

and performance, ensuring a more relevant and engaging learning experience.

6. Talent exchanges with startups: Promote partnerships for talent exchange with startups, allowing employees to work on short-term projects with startups to develop new skills, experience entrepreneurial cultures, and introduce fresh perspectives to their original organisations.

7. Apprenticeships and internships for reskilled employees: Offer structured apprenticeships and internships for employees who have undergone reskilling. This approach provides them with valuable on-the-job training and real-world experience in their new fields. Such programs enable employees to apply their newly acquired skills in practical settings, facilitating smoother transitions into their new roles within the organisation and ensuring the effectiveness of the reskilling efforts.

By incorporating these innovative reskilling techniques, organisations not only invest in the continuous development of their workforce but also adapt to the rapidly changing business landscape, ensuring that their employees remain competitive and their operations stay relevant.

Challenges and solutions

- Engagement and motivation: Combat waning motivation by incorporating engaging learning methods, recognising and rewarding progress, and aligning reskilling with personal career goals.

- Resource constraints: Address limited resources by prioritising key skill areas, leveraging cost-effective online platforms, and adopting scalable learning technologies.
- Measurement of ROI: Overcome challenges in measuring ROI by defining clear metrics for success, such as increased productivity, innovation contributions, and reduced skill gaps.
- Ensuring equity: Ensure equitable access to reskilling opportunities by providing diverse learning modalities, addressing barriers to participation, and actively promoting inclusion.

As organisations embark on the journey of implementing reskilling frameworks, the emphasis should be on flexibility, innovation, and inclusivity. By adopting a strategic approach to reskilling, grounded in a deep understanding of future skill requirements, and supported by a culture of continuous learning, organisations can prepare their workforce not just to navigate the challenges of the digital era but to thrive in them. The success of these frameworks hinge on their adaptability, their capacity to inspire and engage learners, and their alignment with both organisational goals and individual aspirations.

CONTINUOUS LEARNING

In today's rapidly evolving business environment, the concept of continuous learning is integral to adaptability and relevance.

This approach ensures that employees remain updated, engaged, and prepared for the myriad challenges posed by technological advancements and shifting market dynamics.

The philosophy

- Lifelong learning: Encouraging a mindset where learning doesn't end after formal education but continues throughout one's professional journey.
- Curiosity cultivation: Fostering an organisational culture that values questions, exploration, and the pursuit of knowledge.
- Adaptive learning: Prioritising flexibility in learning paths, allowing employees to pivot based on changing industry needs and personal interests.

Digital platforms

- E-learning modules: Using online platforms and courses that allow employees to learn at their own pace.
- Webinars and virtual conferences: Offering opportunities for employees to engage with industry leaders and experts from across the globe.
- Knowledge repositories: Creating digital libraries or databases filled with resources, papers, and case studies for employees to access and learn from.

Collaborative initiatives

- Workshops: Organising in-house workshops where teams can learn new skills or refine existing ones together.
- Team learning challenges: Introducing gamified challenges that promote team-based learning and problem-solving.

- Cross-functional projects: Allowing employees from different departments to collaborate, leading to skill and knowledge exchange.

Feedback and evolution

- Post-training surveys: Collecting feedback from employees after training sessions to continuously refine the learning modules.
- Skill tracking: Using analytics to track the upskilling progress of employees over time.
- Iterative learning pathways: Modifying and updating learning paths based on changing business needs and feedback.

Role of leadership

- Lead by example: Ensuring that top leadership is also engaged in continuous learning, setting a precedent for the entire organisation.
- Open conversations: Ensuring leaders actively discuss their own learning journeys, highlighting the importance of staying updated.
- Resource allocation: Committing organisational resources, both time and financial, towards promoting a culture of continuous learning.

A commitment to continuous learning is more than just a strategy; it's a philosophy that can propel organisations forward in this digital age. By making learning a constant endeavour, businesses can ensure they remain ahead of the curve, with a workforce that's both skilled and motivated.

GLOBAL BEST PRACTICE: GOOGLE'S IT CERTIFICATIONS

Google, a behemoth in the tech industry, has consistently been at the forefront of innovative practices, not only in its products but also in its approach to workforce development. A case in point is Google's IT certifications, which are part of the company's Grow with Google initiative aimed at creating pathways to professional roles in the realm of technology.

Overview of the certification program

- Objective: The program was conceived with a vision to equip individuals, even those without prior tech experience, with foundational IT skills that can lead to job opportunities or further specialisation.
- Accessibility: Google made this program available on the Coursera platform, making it accessible to a vast number of people worldwide.
- Duration: Typically, the certification can be completed in about six months, even without prior IT knowledge, emphasising its beginner-friendly approach.

Curriculum insights

- Broad-based learning: The program covers topics from troubleshooting and customer service, networking, operating systems, and system administration to automation.

- Real-world problem-solving: Learners engage with a mix of hands-on labs and other interactive assessments, ensuring practical application of the acquired knowledge.
- Skill validation: On successful completion, participants receive a professional certificate which is widely recognised by industry leaders, affirming the practical skills and knowledge they've gained.

Impact and outcomes

- Tangible results: Many participants, upon completion, have transitioned into IT roles in various companies, with some even being hired at Google.
- Industry collaboration: Google collaborates with top employers, including Walmart, Best Buy, and Bank of America, ensuring that the program is in sync with industry needs and creates avenues for job placements for the certified individuals.
- Scalability: The online nature of the program means it can cater to a large number of students simultaneously, making high-quality IT education scalable and democratised.

Lessons for organisations

- Customised training: Organisations can take inspiration from Google's IT certifications and tailor training programs that cater to the unique requirements of their industry or business context.
- Collaboration is key: Building partnerships with universities, online platforms, and other businesses

can lead to richer, more industry-relevant training modules.

- Validation matters: Providing a certification or recognition at the end validates the skills and boosts the morale and confidence of the workforce.

Google's IT certifications offer a stellar example of how a well-structured, accessible, and industry-aligned program can bridge the skills gap efficiently. It serves as a reminder to CEOs that with the right approach, they can cultivate a competent, future-ready workforce in-house, fostering both individual and organisational growth.

FRAMEWORK: THE EMPLOYEE TRANSITION LADDER

In the age of rapid digital transformation, transitioning employees through skill evolutions can be visualised as climbing a ladder – each rung representing a progressive step to achieve a higher level of competency and adaptability.

Awareness

- Problem recognition: Employees first understand the nature and magnitude of the skill gap they possess.
- Industry trends: Employees familiarise themselves with the emerging trends in the industry which dictate the skills in demand.

- Self-assessment: Employees evaluate their current skills against what's needed.

Willingness

- Attitude shift: A conscious shift from a fixed mindset to a growth mindset, acknowledging the need for continuous learning.
- Seeking opportunities: Employees proactively seek out training and reskilling opportunities.
- Engagement: Engaging in discussions, forums, and communities focused on skills enhancement.

Ability

- Training: Enrolling in courses, workshops, or seminars pertinent to their skill enhancement.
- Practical application: Implementing learnt skills in real-time projects or assignments to solidify understanding.
- Feedback and iteration: Improving through feedback from peers, mentors, or superiors.

Mastery

- Expertise: Achieving a level of competence where one not only understands the skill but can also innovate using it.
- Mentoring: Guiding and coaching other employees, transferring knowledge.
- Staying updated: Updating oneself regularly with the latest in the domain to maintain the master status.

Contribution

- Collaboration: Collaborating with teams and departments to integrate and leverage the skill.
- Thought leadership: Sharing insights, authoring articles, or speaking at events to influence a wider audience.
- Guiding strategy: Influencing organisational strategy based on the expertise, ensuring the company stays ahead in the competitive landscape.

The transition ladder serves as a structured approach to the employee journey to help employees and organisations understand where they currently stand and what steps they need to take next. It emphasises that skill enhancement is not a destination but a journey that requires constant effort and progression.

FRAMEWORK: THE RESKILLING FUNNEL

The concept of reskilling isn't just about imparting new skills; it's about the strategic approach behind identifying which skills to develop, for whom, and how. Much like the marketing funnel, which moves from awareness to conversion, the reskilling funnel is a structured process that aids organisations in categorising employees based on their current capabilities and the potential for growth within the digital domain.

Identification (top of the funnel)

- Skill audits: Before any reskilling efforts can take place, organisations must first understand where their employees stand. This involves an exhaustive assessment of current skillsets, strengths, and areas for improvement.
- Industry benchmarking: Understand where the industry is heading and the key skills that will be in demand in the near future.

Segmentation (middle of the funnel)

- Rapid adapters: These are individuals who have shown a proclivity for quickly adapting to new tools, technologies, or methodologies.
- Skill enhancers: Employees who possess foundational knowledge but need a deeper dive into more specialised areas.
- Digital novices: Those who are at the start of their digital journey and need significant handholding through the basics.

Customised interventions (narrowing of the funnel)

- For rapid adapters: Advanced workshops, exposure to cutting-edge technologies, or even sponsored courses from leading institutions.
- For skill enhancers: Intermediate courses, cross-training opportunities, or project-based learning.
- For digital novices: Introduction to digital literacy, basic software courses, or mentorship programs.

Evaluation and feedback (bottom of the funnel)

- Skill application: Assess how well the newly acquired skills are being applied in real-world scenarios.
- Feedback mechanism: Create avenues for employees to give feedback on the reskilling initiatives, ensuring future programs are even more tailored and effective.
- Continuous monitoring: Check on changes in the digital landscape regularly to ensure that the workforce remains at the forefront of this change and revisit the funnel periodically.

Scaling and repetition

- Expand programs: After the initial pilot phases, successful programs can be scaled to cover broader segments of the organisation.
- Adopt an iterative approach: Based on the feedback and the outcomes from the initial phases, the reskilling funnel should be seen as an iterative model, constantly evolving based on needs and results.

The reskilling funnel serves as a systematic guide to ensure that reskilling efforts have not adopted a scattergun approach but are strategic and focused and yield tangible results. The below case study illustrates its real-world application in financial services.

GLOBAL BEST PRACTICE: THE RESKILLING FUNNEL APPLIED TO TRANSFORMING A FINANCIAL INSTITUTION'S WORKFORCE

Introduction

A major United States banking and financial services company faced the challenge of reskilling its workforce to adapt to rapidly changing business demands and promote diversity and inclusion within the organisation. This case study explores the innovative approach the company took to address these challenges and achieve significant results.

Challenge

- The bank needed to reskill its workforce to align with emerging job sectors crucial for business success.
- Limited talent pools and the inability to hire a large number of new employees posed a significant hurdle.
- The bank aimed to support its employees in preparing for economic changes, enhance engagement, and promote underrepresented groups.

Solution

The bank adopted a unique funnel approach to reskilling:

FIGURE 8. DEGREED

Reskilling Funnel

The bank used three tiers to allow some workers to explore new possibilities, to help others build foundational new skills, and to support a select few as they took on completely new projects.

Participants
400

Opportunity
Workers invited for new reskilling initiative

150

Tier One:
Participants spent one month testing out the Pathways, which were all about context and self-assessment.

75

Tier Two:
Participants picked one of two selected tracks to begin a five-month reskilling bootcamp.

12

Tier Three:
Top performers from the bootcamps received real projects, engaging their newly acquired skills.

Tier one (broad opening)

- 400 employees at a local site were invited to join the reskilling initiative.
- Approximately one-third (150 employees) opted in for Tier one.
- Participants explored pathways on the learning and upskilling platform, Degreed, to assess their transferable skills and learn about potential career tracks.
- Face-to-face events and networking activities were organised to build engagement and introduce the Degreed platform.

Tier two (narrowing the funnel)

- After one month of exploration, participants had to choose between digital product management or front-end web development tracks.
- Around 50% of participants dropped out at this stage.
- The remaining participants embarked on a five-month reskilling bootcamp, with the help of Degreed pathways.
- In-person panels of professionals in these fields provided insights and advice on career transitions.
- Progress was tracked, and high performers were identified.

Tier three (final selection)

- The top 12 performers from the bootcamps were selected based on data from Degreed.
- They received real projects to apply their newly acquired skills, with mentorship from subject-matter experts.
- The bank celebrated the progress and achievements of all participants.

Results

- Positive indicators included a 16% increase in engagement scores related to job skills and a 20% increase in digital knowledge and skills.
- The company made significant progress towards its diversity goals, with 77% of participants being female and 30% underrepresented minorities.
- The approach proved cost-effective, as investments were made progressively as participants demonstrated commitment and interest.

By implementing a funnel approach to reskilling, the financial institution successfully addressed its challenges. It not only enhanced the skills of its workforce but also improved engagement and diversity within the organisation. This innovative approach demonstrates the importance of tailored reskilling strategies in today's dynamic business landscape.

Transitioning from Chapter 12, which focused on the methodologies and strategies for equipping the workforce with the necessary skills for an evolving digital landscape, Chapter 13 takes a more holistic approach, encompassing skill development as well as adaptive strategies, innovations, and structural changes required for an organisation to thrive in the future.

CHAPTER 13

FUTURE-PROOFING YOUR ORGANISATION

In the face of relentless technological advancements and global interconnectedness, securing an organisation's ability to adapt is paramount. Future-proofing transcends the mere adoption of the latest technologies; it requires cultivating an organisation that can evolve amid an array of future scenarios. This chapter delves into the strategies, methodologies, and mindset shifts crucial for establishing a resilient, adaptive, and forward-thinking organisation.

1. Anticipating and adapting to future trends

- Industry analysis: Dissect industry reports regularly to apprehend emerging trends and the direction of market winds.
- Engaging futurists: Collaborate with forecast experts to gain insights into potential future trends and their impacts.

2. Fostering a culture of innovation

- Internal innovation hubs: Encourage in-house innovation teams to discover new solutions and enhance existing processes.

- Open innovation and co-creation: Establish platforms for collaborative solution generation with external partners and customers.
- Strategic partnerships: Form alliances with startups and other industry entities to amplify innovative capabilities.

3. Organisational flexibility and decision-making

- Decentralised decision-making: Empower individuals and teams to make decisions, ensuring quick response times and adaptability.
- Cross-functional teams: Foster interdisciplinary collaboration for a holistic approach to problem-solving and innovation.

4. Investing in people

- Continuous learning plans: Devise long-term learning roadmaps ensuring employees are equipped with necessary and evolving skills.
- Growth mindset cultivation: Encourage a culture of continuous improvement, learning from failures, and adaptability.

5. Technological preparedness

- Digital transformation: Embrace digital technologies to optimise operations, enhance customer experiences, and drive competitive advantage.

- Modular IT systems: Adopt systems that can be seamlessly upgraded or modified as technology progresses.
- Cybersecurity investments: Allocate resources to fortify organisational and customer data security.

6. Regulatory compliance and ethical practices

- Stay updated with regulatory changes and maintain strict adherence to ethical practices to mitigate legal risks and uphold a reputable brand image.

7. Sustainability and social responsibility

- Environmentally conscious operations: Transition to sustainable practices for better positioning among stakeholders and a positive societal impact.
- Community engagement: Engage in community and social welfare projects to foster a responsible brand image and bolster customer trust.

8. Customer-centricity

- Feedback loops: Develop mechanisms to gather regular feedback from customers, thereby understanding market shifts and improving products/services accordingly.
- Customer-experience enhancement: Invest in improving customer experiences by understanding and anticipating their needs, leveraging data analytics, and applying insights.

9. Diversity and inclusion

- Cultivate a diverse and inclusive workforce to drive innovation, improve decision-making, and better reflect the diverse markets served.

10. Measurement, evaluation, and feedback

- Performance indicators: Establish KPIs and regular review mechanisms to measure the effectiveness of future-proofing strategies.
- Continuous improvement: Utilise feedback from employees, customers, and other stakeholders to drive organisational improvements.

11. Crisis management and resilience-building

- Formulate robust crisis management plans, ensuring organisational survival and recovery from unforeseen adversities.

12. Change management

- Employ effective change management strategies to facilitate smooth transitions during organisational or technological shifts, minimising resistance and maximising acceptance.

Future-proofing is an enduring endeavour requiring an amalgam of proactive strategies, continuous learning, and

FUTURE-PROOFING YOUR ORGANISATION

adaptability. By embracing a forward-focused vision and aligning resources strategically, organisations can navigate the complexities of an ever-changing global landscape, ensuring their relevance, efficacy, and impact in the long run.

GLOBAL BEST PRACTICE: MICROSOFT'S EVOLUTION

The journey of Microsoft, from its inception as a software company to a global technology leader with diverse offerings, stands as a testament to the importance of future-proofing an organisation. Their ability to anticipate change, adapt, and reinvent themselves has kept them at the forefront of the tech industry.

Early days and dominance in personal computing

- Operating system prowess: Microsoft's strategic move in the 1980s with MS-DOS, and later Windows, set them up as the dominant force in the personal computing revolution. By making software that was user-friendly and widely accessible, they captured a massive share of the market.

Navigating the internet wave

- Missed opportunities: Microsoft was initially slow to recognise the potential of the internet, with competitors like Netscape taking an early lead in the browser wars.

- Comeback with Internet Explorer: They eventually rallied, integrating Internet Explorer with the Windows OS, which led to significant market dominance in the browser space by the early 2000s.

The shift to cloud and services

- Recognising the future: As the world started moving towards cloud-based solutions and services, Microsoft, under the leadership of Satya Nadella, pivoted their core strategy.
- Azure and Office 365: Investing heavily in Azure cloud services and transitioning Office to a cloud-based subscription model with Office 365 showcased their commitment to staying ahead of industry trends.

Embracing open source

- A change in philosophy: Historically seen as opposing open source, Microsoft's acquisition of GitHub, a platform central to the open-source community, and making their own tools open source, such as Visual Studio Code, marked a dramatic shift in their approach.
- Benefits: This move earned them goodwill in the developer community and positioned them as champions of the collaborative, open-source development ecosystem.

Continued innovation

- Diverse investments: Microsoft's ventures into AI with products like Azure AI, MR with HoloLens,

and quantum computing show their ongoing commitment to exploring and leading in emerging tech
fields.
- Strategic acquisitions: Purchases such as LinkedIn,
  Mojang (the studio behind Minecraft), and Nuance
  Communications indicate their intention to diversify
  their portfolio and remain relevant across different
  tech domains.

Microsoft's evolution underscores the importance of
adaptability, foresight, and a willingness to change even
when a company is at the top of its game. Their journey
offers valuable lessons for leaders on the significance of
future-proofing their organisations by being receptive to
change, embracing innovation, and taking calculated
risks.

In Chapter 13 we discussed the multifaceted approach to
future-proofing an organisation, encompassing technological
preparedness, fostering innovation, embracing sustainability,
and prioritising customer-centricity and workforce diversity.
This chapter emphasised the importance of an agile, forward-thinking mindset in navigating the complexities of the
modern business landscape. Next, in Chapter 14, we bring
together the key insights from each chapter, offering a holistic
view of the challenges and opportunities inherent in aligning
nationalisation goals with digital transformation. Chapter 13
serves as a reflection on the journey through various strategic perspectives, from understanding the digital skills gap to

implementing effective reskilling frameworks. It underscores the necessity of a human-centric approach, strategic partnerships, and a culture of continuous learning and innovation.

In conclusion, Chapter 14 provides a summary of the book's key takeaways as well as serving as a call to action for leaders in the GCC region. It encourages them to embark on a transformative journey, leveraging the insights and strategies discussed to shape a future where nationalisation objectives and digital prowess work in tandem to foster growth, innovation, and shared prosperity.

CONCLUSION

In the era of rapid digitalisation and shifting economic landscapes, the challenges facing leaders in the GCC region are manifold. The convergence of nationalisation goals and the pressing need for digital competency creates a complex maze that organisations must navigate to remain relevant and competitive.

The journey through this book has explored understanding the nuances of these challenges and offering strategic tools, frameworks, and best practices from around the world. From understanding the origins and aims of nationalisation in the GCC to dissecting the intricacies of the digital skills gap, we've woven a comprehensive tapestry of knowledge and actionable insights.

Key takeaways

1. Harmony between nationalisation and digitalisation: It's imperative to find a balanced approach that honours the nationalisation goals of the GCC while also ensuring organisations remain digitally agile.

2. Human-centric approach: Technology should augment human capabilities, not replace them. Fostering a culture of continuous learning and reskilling is essential for the future workforce.

3. Strategic partnerships: Collaboration between the corporate world, academia, governments, the private sector, and startups can expedite the process of bridging skill gaps and meeting nationalisation objectives.

4. Innovation and adaptability: In a dynamic world, static strategies are doomed to fail. Organisations must inculcate a culture of innovation and be ready to pivot as per market demands.

5. Empowerment: Leaders must empower their teams with the right tools, knowledge, and resources. This is the bedrock on which future success will be built.

As the curtain falls on this playbook, it's important to remember that the journey of digital transformation and aligning with nationalisation goals is continuous. The frameworks and strategies provided are tools to aid in this voyage, but the true compass lies in the vision, determination, and adaptability of the organisation's leadership. It's a journey towards a brighter, more inclusive future, where technology and human potential coalesce to create unprecedented value and opportunities.

SYNTHESIS

The duality of navigating nationalisation while addressing the digital skills gap is a defining challenge for leaders in the GCC region. Throughout this playbook, we've dissected these seemingly parallel tracks, exploring their intersections and providing actionable solutions. Here's a synthesised overview of our journey:

1. Historical foundation: Nationalisation isn't a mere policy directive; it's rooted in the socioeconomic ambitions of the GCC nations. The journey began with understanding its genesis and global precedents.

2. Digital disruption: The wave of digital transformation is reshaping industries globally. We identified the pivotal technologies and the consequent skills they demand.

3. Converging paths: The core revelation was recognising that nationalisation and digital readiness aren't opposing forces. With strategic planning, they can be symbiotic, propelling organisations forward.

4. Global learning: Extracting insights from international case studies, from Estonia's blockchain adoption to AT&T's reskilling initiatives, provided a global perspective on tackling localised challenges.

5. Frameworks for success: Each chapter introduced structured tools and frameworks, from the future-proofing human capital development to the reskilling funnel. These aren't mere theoretical constructs but actionable tools for organisations to apply.

6. The human touch: Amid all the strategy and technology discussions, a recurring theme was the indispensable value of human capital. The focus remained on elevating human potential through continuous learning and fostering collaboration between people and machines.

In essence, the synthesis of this playbook's insights posits that with informed strategies, tenacious execution, and a commitment to both national goals and technological advancement, the future of the GCC's corporate landscape is not just promising but pioneering.

THE CEO'S ACTION PLAN

The roadmap to aligning nationalisation ambitions with digital skills development is multifaceted. Drawing from our comprehensive analysis, here's a distilled action plan tailored for leaders:

1. Vision-crafting: Begin with a clear articulation of your organisation's role in supporting nationalisation and its commitment to embracing the digital era.

2. Data-driven diagnostics: Conduct a thorough skills audit to determine where your organisation currently stands in terms of digital proficiency and alignment with nationalisation goals.

3. Engage and collaborate: Partner with educational institutions, tech incubators, and global thought leaders to harness knowledge and resources. Collaborations can yield tailored training programs, internships, and innovation hubs.

4. Invest in continuous learning: Make reskilling and upskilling a non-negotiable part of your organisation's culture. Consider initiatives like mentorship programs, digital bootcamps, and rotational assignments.

5. Embrace technology: Prioritise investments in core technologies identified in Chapter 6. Remember, it's not about chasing every tech trend but aligning tech adoption with your strategic goals.

6. Feedback loops: Foster a culture where feedback, from employees at all levels and from external stakeholders, is not only encouraged but actively sought. This will keep your strategies agile and adaptive.

7. Celebrate successes: Recognise and reward both individual and collective achievements that further your twin goals. This boosts morale and drives engagement.

8. Community engagement: Engage with the community to reinforce your organisation's commitment to national development and technological progress.

Incorporating these action points into your leadership strategy will help you navigate the intersecting paths of nationalisation and digital transformation and set your organisation on a trajectory of sustained growth and impact.

CLOSING REMARKS

In the rapidly evolving world of business, challenges are inevitable. The intricacies between nationalisation and the burgeoning digital skills gap present a unique conundrum, particularly for the GCC region. Yet, these challenges also offer an unmatched opportunity – a chance to shape the future of the workforce, influence economic directions, and carve a legacy built on foresight and innovation.

It's pertinent to remember that the interplay between nationalisation goals and digital readiness isn't about finding a short-term compromise. Instead, it's about crafting a harmonious synthesis that uplifts both mandates, ensuring that they complement and amplify each other. As leaders, your role is pivotal. The responsibility is weighty, but so are the potential rewards.

The paths laid out in this playbook aren't merely transactional strategies; they represent a transformative journey. A journey that, when undertaken with diligence, vision, and empathy, has the potential to impact not just organisations or industries, but entire nations.

I urge you to embrace this journey with an open heart and a resolute mind. The future beckons, and it promises a horizon where nationalisation and digital prowess walk hand in hand, shaping a world of opportunities, growth, and shared prosperity.

Let this book be your guiding compass, helping you navigate the challenges and seize the potential that lies ahead.

AUTHOR BIO

Dua **Al Toobi** is a visionary leader in digital transfor-mation and human capital development, known for her expertise in bridging the digital skills gap across the GCC. With a career spanning the banking, aviation, and semi-government sectors, she has led large-scale mergers, organi-zational transformations, and strategic workforce initiatives. Her unique experience in both digital transformation and HR leadership positions her at the intersection of technology, talent, and change.

As the founder of **The Future-Proof Advisory**, Dua partners with government bodies and enterprises to design people-first workforce strategies that align with the demands of tomor-row's economy. A former Director of Digital Transformation and Head of HR responsible for Organisational Development, HR Transformation, and Culture, she has helped future-proof organizations by integrating emerging technologies with national workforce priorities.

Beyond the boardroom, Dua is a well-known TV presenter, demystifying complex tech trends for everyday audiences and fostering accessible conversations around innovation. A respected speaker and academic, she holds an Executive Master in Digital Transformation and is pursuing a Doctorate of Business Administration with a focus on future-proofing GCC workforces.

Her book, *Future-Proof Your Workforce: Bridging the Divide Between Nationalisation Goals and the Digital Skills Gap in the GCC – A Leader's Playbook*, offers a strategic and actionable guide for leaders navigating transformation in both the public and private sectors.

When she's not advising executives or speaking on global stages, Dua is passionate about adventure and personal growth – with a love for travel, cycling, boxing, and scuba diving.

LET'S BUILD THE FUTURE TOGETHER

As you reach the final pages of *Future-Proof Your Workforce: Bridging the Divide Between Nationalisation Goals and the Digital Skills Gap in the GCC – A Leader's Playbook*, I want to thank you for being part of this journey. The future of work is no longer approaching – it's already here. And with it comes the responsibility, and the opportunity, to lead transformation that is both human and future-focused.

Whether you're shaping national workforce strategies, leading digital transformation within your organization, or navigating your own career pivot, now is the time to act. The systems we build today will define the economy, workforce, and society of tomorrow.

Through **The Future-Proof Advisory**, I work with leaders ready to turn vision into action. Our work spans strategic advisory, thought leadership, education, and impact – all rooted in people-first transformation.

Our core pillars include:

- **Advisory & Consulting**
  Strategic guidance for governments and enterprises to align digital disruption with workforce reskilling and national goals.
- **Thought Leadership & Media**
  Keynotes, panels, media platforms, and public engagement to demystify the future of work and inspire system-level change.
- **Education & Tools**
  Scalable courses and toolkits designed to support reskilling, career transitions, and organisational workforce development.
- **Impact & Research**
  Collaborations with leading institutions to publish data-driven insights on skills gaps, transformation ROI, and nationalisation strategies.

This book is only the beginning. If you're ready to take the next step toward building a resilient, inclusive, and future-ready workforce – I invite you to connect, collaborate, and explore what's possible.

➤ Learn more at www.thefutureproofadvisory.com

LET'S CONNECT:

✉ **Email:** connect@duaaltoobi.com
🌐 **Website:** www.duaaltoobi.com
💼 **LinkedIn:** @duaaltoobi
📱 **Instagram:** @dua_altoobi

Together, we can bridge the gap between potential and achievement, navigating the challenges of today to shape the successes of tomorrow.

The future belongs to those who are prepared – let's build it, together.

WORKS CITED

Accenture. (2018, October 24). *Advancing human-AI collaboration.* https://www.accenture.com/us-en/insights/future-workforce/missing-middle-skills-human-ai-collaboration

Business Finland. (2021). *TechSkillsAtlas 2021.* https://www.business finland.fi/49743f/globalassets/julkaisut/invest-in-finland/fin-land-techskillsatlas-2021_web.pdf

Degreed. (2022, October 2). *Taking skills to the bank.* https://get.degreed.com/hubfs/Degreed%20Case%20Studies/Anonymous_Reskilling_Case%20Study_04302020.pdf?utm_campaign=DOC-CASE-Degreed-LXP-ENG-AnonymousBank-8_23&utm_medium=email&_hsmi=86649122&_hsenc=p2ANqtz-8HMHQU8206iEHxl82SNr0UDpZmlw11aDXHRd4CmKWHb2usY_Ls

Deloitte Insights. (2022, November 22). *Human-machine collaboration.* https://www2.deloitte.com/xe/en/insights/topics/talent/human-machine-collaboration.html

EU Digital Skills & Jobs Platform. (2022). *Finland's digital progress programme.* Publications Office of the European Union. https://digital-skills-jobs.europa.eu/en/latest/briefs/finland-snapshot-digital-skills

Government of Saudi Arabia. (n.d.). *Saudi Vision 2030.* https://www.vision2030.gov.sa/en/

Government of Singapore. (n.d.). *SkillsFuture.* https://www.skillsfuture.gov.sg

Government of the People's Republic of China. (2017). *New generation artificial intelligence development plan* (G. Webster et al, trans.). https://digichina.stanford.edu/work/full-translation-chinas-new-generation-artificial-intelligence-development-plan-2017

IBM Newsroom. (2020, November 17). *IBM makes education & hiring more inclusive worldwide with P-TECH model expanding across 28 countries.* https://newsroom.ibm.com/2020-11-17-IBM-Makes-Education-Hiring-More-Inclusive-Worldwide-with-P-TECH-Model-Expanding-Across-28-Countries

Kerr, W. & Kreitzberg, C. (2019, July). *AT&T, retraining, and the workforce of tomorrow.* Harvard Business School Case 820-017. (Revised May 2020.)

Korn Ferry. (n.d.). *The $8.5 trillion talent shortage.* https://www.kornferry.com/insights/this-week-in-leadership/talent-crunch-future-of-work

World Economic Forum. (2020). *The future of jobs report 2020.* https://www3.weforum.org/docs/WEF_Future_of_Jobs_2020.pdf

World Economic Forum. (n.d.) The Fourth Industrial Revolution, by Klaus Schwab. https://www.weforum.org/about/the-fourth-industrial-revolution-by-klaus-schwab/

https://reports.weforum.org/docs/WEF_Future_of_Jobs_Report_2025.pdf

NOTES